# THE COMPLETE BOOK OF
# HOME
# BAKING

## HEILIE PIENAAR

NEW
HOLLAND

## ACKNOWLEDGEMENTS

I wish to express my gratitude to Rob Opie and Wendy Botha at Premier Foods, for the opportunity given to me to use such a versatile product range for creating these exciting recipes and for helping to make this book possible. To my family and friends, for all their support, encouragement, and tasting throughout the months of recipe testing. To Annelie and Carol, who assisted with the baking for photo shoots, and to Brandon for his magnificent photography. And lastly but so important, the publishing team: Linda de Villiers, for believing so strongly in the Snowflake brand, Joy Clack for her utmost patience with editing and Bev Dodd for the beautiful layout.

Many thanks also go to Yellow Door (Tygervalley and Gardens centers) for some beautiful props, to Nettie for painting special plates, and to William for the use of his house during photography.

HEILIE PIENAAR, 2002

First published in 2002 by
New Holland Publishers (UK) Ltd
This edition published 2003
Garfield House
86-88 Edgware Road
London W2 2EA
London • Cape Town • Sydney • Auckland

www.newhollandpublishers.com

1 2 3 4 5 6 7 8 9 10

PUBLISHING MANAGER: Linda de Villiers
RECIPE DEVELOPER: Heilie Pienaar
EDITOR: Joy Clack
DESIGNER: Beverley Dodd
COVER DESIGNER: Sean Robertson
PHOTOGRAPHER: Brandon Amron-Coetzee
STYLIST: Heilie Pienaar

Reproduction by Hirt & Carter Cape (Pty) Ltd
Printed and bound by Times Offset (M) Sdn Bhd

ISBN 1 84330 561 5

EGGS: Because of the slight risk of salmonella, raw eggs should not be served to the very young, the ill or elderly or to pregnant women.

ROYAL ICING (PAGE 106): use a dried egg white substitute.
MARZIPAN (PAGE 106): if you are concerned about the raw egg content in this recipe, use a ready-made marzipan.

# CONTENTS

INTRODUCTION  4

COOKIES AND RUSKS  10

BARS, SQUARES, AND SWEET TREATS  22

QUICK LOAVES AND LARGE CAKES  30

BREADS  46

SWEET TARTS AND PIES  58

MUFFINS AND SCONES  70

PIES AND MAIN COURSE BAKES  80

DESSERTS  96

CELEBRATIONS  106

KIDS  116

MISTAKES AND CAUSES  124

GLOSSARY  125

INDEX  127

# INTRODUCTION

*This book is mainly about traditional baking. The basic recipes for biscuits, cakes, breads, muffins, and so on are here, but are sometimes presented in a novel way. Admittedly, some of the recipes are not low in fat, but then again, we are all allowed to enjoy something sweet now and again.*

## INGREDIENTS

All ingredients should be at room temperature, unless otherwise stated.

### Flour

Flour, milled from bread wheats, is the major ingredient used in most baking. It must be of an adequate protein (gluten) strength to:

- form an elastic, extensible dough;
- withstand mixing, stretching, and shaping;
- support the weight of other ingredients.

Wheat grain comprises three main parts.

- The bran coating is 14–15% and contains a high proportion of fiber, which aids digestion and prevents constipation. This outer shell is removed to produce white flour.
- The endosperm (inner part of the kernel) is 80–84%. It consists of protein and starch, which are important for energy. White flour is milled from the endosperm.
- The germ is 2–3%. It is present in whole-wheat flour, and is milled separately to produce wheatgerm.

Bread flour provides the vital protein needed for bread and pizza doughs. It is the protein that forms gluten when the flour is mixed with liquid to make a dough; the gluten becomes elastic and traps the carbon dioxide gas released as the dough ferments. This causes the dough to rise. If a lighter end product with a softer crumb is desired, a cake for example, a "softer" flour, lower in protein content, should be used.

### Storing

White flours can be stored for up to eight months in cool conditions, or up to a year in a refrigerator or freezer. Bran and whole-wheat and brown flours, which can become rancid due to their high bran content, should only be stored for up to three months. Note the following to ensure that flour is maintained in optimum condition:

- Store in an airtight container in a cool, dry place, away from products with strong flavors or odors.
- Do not add fresh flour to old when refilling containers.
- Place a bay leaf in the flour to discourage insect infestation.
- Take note of the "best before" date stamped on the package.
- The age of flour, and thus its moisture content, will determine the amount of liquid to be used. The fresher the flour, the less liquid is required. Humidity in the environment will also have an effect. Add liquid gradually, not all at once.

### Types of flour

A wide variety of flours is available for cooking and baking, and getting to know the characteristics of each flour will help to ensure you use the right one for the purpose.

Broadly speaking, flours are defined by the quantities of the wheats used and their rate of extraction. The extraction is the percentage of whole, cleaned wheatgrain in the flour. There are three basic flour categories:

- whole-wheat, with 100% extraction, made from the whole wheatgrain with nothing added and nothing taken away;
- brown, with about 85% extraction, as some bran and germ are removed;
- white, usually with 75% extraction, because most of the bran and germ are removed during milling.

Stoneground flour is whole-wheat flour ground in a traditional way between two stones, rather than using modern factory rollers. It is usually coarser and heavier than factory-milled flour and is more nutritious because it retains more B vitamins.

Organic flours are milled from grain grown without artificial fertilizers or pesticides on organic farms.

### All-purpose flour

All-purpose flour, which may be white, brown, or whole-wheat, is the most widely used. It is milled from a variety of hard and soft wheats, and its protein content usually ranges from seven to ten percent. All-purpose flour is ideal for cakes, cookies, most pastries, and general cooking, such as coating food and thickening sauces.

Clockwise from top left: *Wheatgerm flour, Bread flour, Brown bread flour, Wheat bran, Semolina, All-purpose flour, Self-rising flour.*

### Self-rising flour

This is white, brown, or whole-wheat flour to which a rising agent has been added to give lightness to the baked product. It is usually used for biscuits, cakes, and cookies, and quick breads or teabreads.

After opening, self-rising flour must be stored in an airtight container to preserve the rising agent. To make your own self-rising flour, add 1 tsp baking powder to each cup of all-purpose flour. Always sift this before using to mix it evenly.

### Bread flour

This is usually white, although brown and whole-wheat bread flours are available. Bread flour has a protein content of 11–14%, which makes it the best flour for yeasted doughs. It is also excellent for making puff pastry.

### Granary flour

Also called malted wheatgrain flour, this is brown flour milled from malted wheat (grains that have been allowed to begin fermenting) to which whole and cracked wheatgrains are added. Granary flour has a distinctive nutty flavor and texture.

### Wheat germ flour

This is white or brown flour with at least 10% wheat germ added to it.

### Spelt flour

Milled from an ancient ancestor of wheat, spelt flour is more nutritious, but contains less protein than modern wheat flour.

### Semolina

Durum wheat, a "hard" wheat with a high protein content, is the source of semolina. It is milled to produce the traditional flour for making pasta. Semolina is also used to make gnocchi (small dumplings) and couscous, as well as milk puddings.

### Wheat bran

The outer layer of the wheat kernel is removed to produce bran, an unrefined by-product of flour. Wheat bran is rich in hemi-cellulose, fiber, vitamins, and minerals and can be added to breads, scones, and granola. It can also be sprinkled over oatmeal and cereal. Store it for three to four months under ideal conditions, and up to a year in a refrigerator or freezer.

### Non-wheat flours

Wheat flour is the most commonly used, but other grains are also milled into flour. These can be blended with wheat flour or used on their own, to give variety to your cooking and baking.

Those that are gluten-free are ideal for people with gluten intolerance.

- barley flour has a sweet nutty flavor; it is low in gluten so not ideal for baking unless mixed with wheat flour;
- buckwheat flour contains no gluten so cannot be used for yeasted doughs. However, it is useful for scones, pancakes and blinis, and flat breads;
- cornmeal has a slightly granular texture and is gluten-free; it is cooked to make polenta and is also used for breads and muffins;
- gram or garbanzo flour is a gluten-free flour traditionally used for chapatis and other flat breads;
- oat flour and oatmeal are used with wheat flour for all sorts of baking;
- rye flour, low in gluten, gives bread a rich flavor and chewy texture;
- soya flour, milled from raw or toasted soya beans, is high in protein but gluten-free.

## Butter

Butter is important for any baking. It gives cakes, cookies and pastries a rich flavor, tenderness, or crispness and a warm subtle color. Sweet butter is preferable for cakes and cookies.

### Storing

Chilled, salted butter keeps well for up to one month and sweet butter for up to two weeks. Butter freezes well for up to six months.

### Baking

It is important to use butter at the correct temperature. For cookies, cakes and breads, use at room temperature for better creaming with sugar.

### Alternatives/substitutions

Margarine can be used instead of butter in most recipes, but the creamy taste of butter is necessary for delicate pastries. If substituting margarine, use the hard, block type. The soft type (tub) has a higher water content and should only be used when mentioned specifically.

## Sugar

### Confectioner's sugar

Almost powdery in texture, confectioner's sugar dissolves immediately. It is used mainly for smooth frostings, but is also excellent for meringues, whipped cream, sifting over pies and desserts and for decorations. Confectioner's sugar is not usually used in cake mixtures as it does not create enough volume when creamed.

### Granulated sugar

This has larger grains than superfine sugar, so if used in delicate cakes it can cause a speckled appearance. It can be used for rubbed-in mixtures such as for cookies, in place of superfine sugar, if preferred.

### Muscovado sugar

Soft and fine in texture, this unrefined sugar may be light or dark. It is used when a rich molasses-type flavor is required, such as in gingerbreads or fruitcakes.

### Raw brown sugar

Deep gold in color, with slightly sticky, large crystals, raw brown is an unrefined sugar derived from raw sugar cane.

## SUBSTITUTING INGREDIENTS

| | |
|---|---|
| 2 sticks (1 cup) butter | scant 1 cup sunflower or other mild oil |
| 1 tbsp cornstarch | 2 tbsp all-purpose flour |
| 1 cup self-rising flour | 1 cup all-purpose flour + 1 tsp baking powder |
| 4 tsp baking powder | 2 tsp cream of tartar + 1 tsp baking soda |
| 1 tsp cream of tartar | 1 tbsp lemon juice or vinegar or $\frac{1}{2}$ tsp tartaric acid |
| 1 tbsp active dry yeast | scant 1 oz fresh yeast |
| 1 cup superfine sugar | 1 cup corn syrup or honey |
| 1 cup soured cream | 1 cup milk + 4 tsp lemon juice or 1 tbsp vinegar |
| 1 cup yogurt | 1 cup buttermilk or sour cream |
| 1 cup cream | $\frac{3}{4}$ cup milk + $\frac{1}{2}$ stick butter or scant $\frac{3}{4}$ cup buttermilk + $\frac{1}{3}$ cup sunflower oil |
| 1 whole egg in cookies and cakes | 2 tbsp water + $\frac{1}{2}$ tsp baking powder or 1 egg white + 2 tsp sunflower oil |
| 1 tsp lemon juice | $\frac{1}{2}$ tsp vinegar |
| 1 oz chocolate | $\frac{1}{4}$ cup unsweetened cocoa + 2 tsp butter |

NB: If you can't find a can of the exact weight specified, use the nearest to it.

### Soft brown sugar

Whether light or dark, this is a refined white sugar colored with syrup or molasses.

### Superfine sugar

This is the kind most used in baking. It is ideal for creaming as well as for whisking with eggs as its fine grains dissolve quickly. Superfine sugar is also used for meringues.

## Eggs

Eggs are indispensable in baking. They can be used whole or separately as yolks and whites to bind a mixture, to add richness and to create volume. All recipes in this book have been tested using large eggs. It is preferable not to use smaller eggs. The color of the shell does not determine the flavor, but size makes a difference.

### Storing

Bake with fresh eggs. Eggs should not be older than 21 days. Refrigerate with pointed ends facing down.

To test if an egg is fresh, immerse it horizontally in cold water. If it is fresh it will sink to the bottom without tilting. If it tilts, it may be up to a week old. If it floats vertically, it is old.

### Baking

Eggs should be at room temperature before baking. If they are too cold the whites won't whisk up to the required volume. When whisking egg whites, ensure that no yolk is present and that the bowl is completely grease-free. Only whisk egg whites just before using as they lose volume quickly. Do not overbeat. Egg yolks, on the other hand, will curdle quickly if they are too cold or if added to a cake mixture too quickly. Add beaten egg a little at a time, and sprinkle in a tablespoon of flour if the mixture starts to curdle.

### Substituting

Eggs are not easy to substitute. In baking, they provide richness, color and protein. Most baking problems start when substituting eggs or fats. Egg whites provide extra volume and air. Eggs are also used for binding.

When substituting eggs, it is important to know the purpose they serve in the recipe. If the recipe calls for one egg, it normally serves as a binding agent. More than three eggs cannot be substituted successfully. In some recipes, for example light sponge cakes, only eggs will do.

## Baking powder

This is a mixture of baking soda, starch, and acids, used to make cakes and some light doughs rise. The acids in the baking powder react with the baking soda when liquid is added, releasing the carbon dioxide that aerates the mixture.

## Baking soda

This reacts with acids such as the cream of tartar in baking powder, or buttermilk and yogurt in a mixture, and releases carbon dioxide. When baking soda is used alone, and not as a component of baking powder, the cake, quick bread, scones, or other items must be baked immediately. Delays will result in a loss of volume. Too much baking soda gives quick breads a soapy flavor with an acid smell. Both baking soda and baking powder have a fine texture and do not need to be dissolved in hot water.

## Yeast

Active dry yeast is a dry yeast to which Vitamin C has been added. Active dry yeast can be mixed directly with flour. If you prefer to use ordinary dry yeast it must be dissolved in tepid water and then left to stand until frothy before being added to the flour.

## TYPES OF PASTRY

### Pie dough

This contains one part fat to two parts flour. Keep ingredients cool, work quickly, and chill pastry before rolling out. Pie dough is used for single-crust pies, quiches, and sweet tarts.

### Rich pie dough

This pastry can be rolled out more thinly than basic pie dough. Egg yolk and sugar are usually added, resulting in a richer pastry that will stay crisp for longer. This pastry is ideal for tartlet shells and is often baked blind.

### Sweet pie dough

This pastry is similar to rich pie dough, with the addition of an extra egg, sugar, and vanilla extract.

### Puff pastry

An equal proportion of fat to flour is usually used to make this pastry. Puff pastry has a texture that is delicate, fine, and flaky, and is ideal for making pie toppings, fine pastries, and tarts.

### Flaky pastry

This is not as delicate as puff pastry, but it is flaky, rises high, and can be used for the same purposes.

## Cream cheese pastry

This rich pastry, made with cream cheese or sieved cottage cheese, can be used in a variety of dishes. The pastry is easy to handle if the ingredients are cold.

## Soda-water pastry

This is a good substitute for puff pastry as it is also made in layers. It is ideal for dessert and main-course dishes.

## Choux pastry

This pastry differs from all others because it is made in a saucepan, is soft, and has to be piped or spooned. Choux pastry should be baked until dry to ensure it holds its shape.

## GENERAL BAKING RULES

- Read the recipe carefully. Make sure you have all the ingredients before you start.
- Measure and weigh ingredients accurately.
- Always sift flour to aerate it.
- Unless otherwise specified, use ingredients at room temperature.
- The correct baking pan is essential. Measure across the top on the inside of the pan.
- As most recipes require a preheated oven, switch on the oven before starting your preparation.

---

## IMPERIAL/METRIC CONVERSION TABLES

All of the recipes in this book have measures in cups and imperial measurements. However, you may find the table below useful if you come across recipes in other books that include metric measurements.

### Volume measures

| | | |
|---|---|---|
| 75 ml (2½ fl oz) | 240 ml (8 fl oz) | 500 ml (17 fl oz) |
| 90 ml (3 fl oz) | 250 ml (8½ fl oz) | 600 ml (1¼ pints) |
| 100 ml (3½ fl oz) | 300 ml (10 fl oz) | 750 ml (1½ pints) |
| 120 ml (4 fl oz) | 360 ml (12 fl oz) | 1 litre (2 pints) |
| 150 ml (5 fl oz) | 400 ml (14 fl oz) | |
| 200 ml (7 fl oz) | 450 ml (15 fl oz) | |

### Weights

| | | | |
|---|---|---|---|
| 10 g (¼ oz) | 115 g (4 oz) | 400 g (14 oz) | 1.25 kg (2¾ lb) |
| 15 g (½ oz) | 125 g (4½ oz) | 450 g (1 lb) | 1.35 kg (3 lb) |
| 20 g (¾ oz) | 140 g (5 oz) | 500 g (1 lb 2 oz) | 1.5 kg (3 lb 3 oz) |
| 25 g (scant 1 oz) | 150 g (5½ oz) | 550 g (1¼ lb) | 1.8 kg (4 lb) |
| 30 g (1 oz) | 170 g (6 oz) | 600 g (1 lb 5 oz) | 2 kg (4½ lb) |
| 45 g (1½ oz) | 200 g (7 oz) | 675 g (1½ lb) | 2.25 kg (5 lb) |
| 50 g (1¾ oz) | 225 g (8 oz) | 750 g (1 lb 10 oz) | 2.5 kg (5½ lb) |
| 55 g (2 oz) | 250 g (8½ oz) | 800 g (1¾ lb) | 2.7 kg (6 lb) |
| 75 g (2½ oz) | 280 g (10 oz) | 900 g (2 lb) | 3 kg (6½ lb) |
| 85 g (3 oz) | 300 g (10½ oz) | 1 kg (2¼ lb) | |
| 100 g (2½ oz) | 340 g (12 oz) | 1.1 kg (2½ lb) | |

### Linear measures

| | | | |
|---|---|---|---|
| 3 mm (⅛ in) | 6 cm (2½ in) | 20 cm (8 in) | 50 cm (20 in) |
| 5 mm (¼ in) | 7.5 cm (3 in) | 23 cm (9 in) | 61 cm (24 in) |
| 1 cm (½ in) | 10 cm (4 in) | 25 cm (10 in) | 77 cm (30 in) |
| 2 cm (¾ in) | 12 cm (5 in) | 28 cm (11 in) | |
| 2.5 cm (1 in) | 15 cm (6 in) | 30 cm (12 in) | |
| 5 cm (2 in) | 18 cm (7 in) | 46 cm (18 in) | |

- The baking times given in each recipe are only to be used as a guide. Ovens and bakeware vary and this can affect the final baking times. Changes in ingredients can also affect the baking time.
- Check cakes 5 minutes before the end of the baking time. Use a cake tester to test if cooked through.

## KITCHEN EQUIPMENT

The most basic equipment is usually enough, although electric mixers and food processors make baking much easier and quicker. Electronic equipment – digital scales for example – are extremely useful as it is advisable to measure some ingredients accurately. Before starting to bake, ensure that you have all the equipment you need.

## BAKING SHEETS/PANS

Nonstick coated or heavy-duty aluminum pans are best as this material distributes the heat evenly. Grease pans with a sprayed-on nonstick coating or a brush dipped in melted butter. Lining pans with waxed paper or baking parchment is also advised.

For best results, always use the size indicated in a recipe to avoid overflowing. A guideline is to fill pans to no more than half to two-thirds full, thus leaving room for expansion.

## OVENS

Always allow a minimum of 1 inch around pans for even heat distribution. When baking on more than one shelf, rearrange the pans halfway through the baking time.

Fan ovens are ideal for baking as a fan circulates the heat inside the oven, resulting in an even temperature throughout. As baking times are often slightly less in a fan oven, adjust the temperature as required.

## Microwave ovens

None of these recipes has been tested in a microwave oven as the cooking times and results are very different from baking in a standard oven.

## OVEN TEMPERATURES

|  | °F | °C |
|---|---|---|
| very cool | 200 | 100 |
| very cool | 250 | 120 |
| cool | 300 | 150 |
| moderate | 325 | 160 |
| moderate | 350 | 180 |
| moderate hot | 375 | 190 |
| hot | 400 | 200 |
| hot | 425 | 220 |
| very hot | 475 | 240 |

## PAN SIZES

Measure across the top, on the inside of the pan.

| | |
|---|---|
| Springform pan, round | 9 inches |
| Cake pan | 8 inches |
| Loose-bottomed cake pan | 9 inches |
| Ring pan | 8¾ inches |
| Deep square cake pan | 8 inches |
| Jelly roll pan | 9 x 13 inches |
| Loaf pan | 9 inches |
| Loose-bottomed tart pan | 9½ inches |
| Fluted tart pan | 9½ inches |
| Pizza pan | 10 inches |
| Square pan | 9½ inches |
| Rectangular pan | 9½ x 14 inches |
| Rectangular pan | 8 x 9½ inches |
| Tray bake pan | 6½ x 10½ inches |

# COOKIES AND RUSKS

## COOKIES

### Ingredients
The quality of the ingredients is always important, yet it is not as critical with cookies as it is with cakes. When baking cookies, many different variations can be achieved by swapping the flavoring ingredients.

### Dropped cookies
The dough is usually very soft and is spooned onto greased cookie sheets. Leave enough space between each cookie to allow room for spreading.

### Rolled cookies
The dough is firm and can therefore be rolled out thinly, to a thickness of about 1/8 inch, before being cut into shapes with a cookie cutter. Roll out the dough on a lightly floured surface —don't use too much flour as this will make the dough tough. If the dough is sticky, roll it out between sheets of waxed paper. Roll in one direction to produce an even thickness.

### Shaped cookies
The dough is usually soft and is forced through a pastry bag fitted with a tip. When firmer dough is used it is shaped by hand or pressed through a cookie maker. It may also be chilled before baking to maintain its shape.

### Refrigerator cookies
The dough is shaped into long sausage forms and is chilled or frozen before being cut into slices with a sharp knife. The slices are then arranged on greased cookie sheets and baked.

### Baking
Leave at least 1 inch between the cookie sheet and the sides of the oven. When using a standard oven, ideally bake one tray of cookies at a time—the best results are achieved using the middle shelf. If baking on more than one cookie sheet, swap their positions halfway through to achieve more even baking. If you are using a fan oven, more cookies can be baked at a time because all oven shelves can be used. Cookies normally bake quickly, 10–15 minutes in total in a moderate oven.

### Cooling and storing
Cookies are normally soft when removed from the oven, but will harden as they cool. The longer they are baked, the harder they will become. Some cookies bake brittle and need to be removed carefully before being placed on wire racks to cool. Make sure that the cookies are cold before storing in an airtight container. They must be stored on their own as they soften quickly and can absorb other flavors.

When unfrosted cookies start to soften they can be crisped again by heating in a moderate oven for about 5 minutes. Hard cookies can be successfully frozen for up to three months, and will defrost within one hour at room temperature.

## CHOCOLATE CHUNK COOKIES

2 sticks butter or 1 cup margarine
½ cup superfine sugar
½ cup light brown sugar
2 large eggs
1 tsp vanilla extract
2 cups self-rising flour
5½ oz semisweet chocolate, coarsely chopped

**1** Cream the butter and both sugars together. Add eggs and vanilla extract and beat well until light and fluffy.

**2** Sift flour and add, mixing well. Stir in chocolate chunks.

**3** Drop teaspoonfuls onto a greased cookie sheet and bake in a preheated oven at 350 °F for 10–12 minutes.

**4** Remove cookies and place on a wire rack to cool.

MAKES ABOUT 60

---

### VARIATION
Substitute chopped chocolate pieces with chocolate chips.

---

### TIP
To make fine crumbs, place any crispy cookies inside a plastic bag and use a rolling pin to crush them until fine.

Chocolate Chunk Cookies

## COTTAGE DELIGHTS

2 cups butter or margarine
generous 1 cup superfine sugar
1 tsp lemon or almond extract
1½ cups condensed milk
5½ cups all-purpose flour
4 tsp baking powder
scant ½ tsp salt

**1** Cream the butter and sugar. Add the lemon or almond extract and condensed milk and beat well.

**2** Sift the remaining ingredients and mix into the butter mixture.

**3** Shape teaspoonfuls of dough into balls. Place on greased cookie sheets and flatten slightly with a fork.

**4** Bake in a preheated oven at 325 °F for 15–20 minutes. Transfer to a wire rack to cool. Store in an airtight container.

MAKES ABOUT 90

### TIPS

- Sprinkle a layer of sugar in the bottom of the storage container to keep cookies or rusks fresh for longer.
- Undecorated cookies that start going soft can be crisped up in the oven at 350 °F for 5 minutes.

## JELLY AND COCONUT COOKIES

2 cups all-purpose flour
2 tsp baking powder
scant ½ tsp salt
¾ cup superfine sugar
1 stick butter or ½ cup margarine
3 large eggs, separated
3 tbsp water
2½ cups smooth apricot jelly
scant 2 cups dry unsweetened coconut

**1** Sift flour, baking powder, and salt. Add 2 tbsp superfine sugar. Rub in butter.

**2** Add egg yolks and water and knead to a soft dough. Roll out to ⅛ inch thick. Stamp out rounds of about scant 3 inch in diameter. Press into greased patty pans. Spoon 2 tsp apricot jelly into each.

**3** Whisk egg whites until stiff and add remaining superfine sugar and coconut. Spoon about 1 tbsp egg white mix over apricot jelly.

**4** Bake in a preheated oven at 350 °F for 20–25 minutes. Remove and cool on a wire rack.

MAKES ABOUT 18

### VARIATION

Substitute apricot jelly with any other flavor jelly.

### TIP

Sprinkle just enough flour on the work counter and rolling pin to prevent sticking. Excess flour may cause the cookies to be hard.

## SHORTBREAD TWIRLS

2 sticks butter or 1 cup margarine
1 tsp vanilla extract
1 tsp almond extract
½ cup superfine sugar
2 cups all-purpose flour
scant ½ tsp salt
1 tbsp milk

**1** Cream butter, both extracts and sugar together until light and fluffy.

**2** Sift flour and salt and add to the mixture, together with the milk.

**3** Spoon the mixture into a pastry bag fitted with a large star tip and pipe decorative shapes onto a greased cookie sheet.

**4** Bake in a preheated oven at 325 °F for 12–15 minutes, or until lightly browned. Transfer to a wire rack to cool.

MAKES ABOUT 20

### VARIATIONS

For chocolate shortbread, omit the milk and add 2 tbsp unsweetened cocoa powder mixed with 2 tbsp hot water to the shortbread mixture. Mix well. Alternatively, dip one side of each cookie into melted chocolate, or drizzle chocolate over the top.

**Left to right:** *Shortbread Twirls, Jelly and Coconut Cookies, Cottage Delights.*

## BUTTERSCOTCH COOKIES

2 sticks butter or 1 cup margarine
2 cups brown sugar
2 large eggs
1 tsp vanilla extract
scant 4 cups all-purpose flour
1 tsp baking powder
½ tsp baking soda
scant 2 cups walnuts or pecans,
chopped

**1** Cream butter and sugar. Add eggs, one at a time, and beat until light and fluffy. Add vanilla extract.

**2** Sift flour, baking powder, and baking soda and add. Add nuts.

**3** Shape into two rolls of 9½ inches in length. Wrap in waxed paper and chill or freeze until hard.

**4** Slice into cookies of ½ inch in thickness and arrange on greased cookie sheets. Bake in a preheated oven at 350 °F for 15–20 minutes until light brown. Transfer to a wire rack to cool.

MAKES ABOUT 50

### VARIATION
Make crumbs from these cookies and use them as a base for a delicious tart. Mix ½ cup melted butter with the crumbs and use as a base for the Ginger and Cherry Tart (page 68).

## RICH ALMOND COOKIES

1 cup all-purpose flour
½ cup cornstarch
¾ cup ground almonds
¼ cup superfine sugar
scant ½ tsp vanilla extract
scant ½ tsp salt
2 sticks soft butter or 1 cup margarine
1 tsp grated lemon rind (optional)
about 3 tbsp confectioner's sugar
for rolling

**1** Sift flour and mix with all other ingredients except confectioner's sugar. Shape teaspoonfuls of mixture into balls and place on greased cookie sheets.

**2** Bake in a preheated oven at 325 °F for 30–35 minutes. Leave to cool slightly. Roll in confectioner's sugar.

MAKES ABOUT 48

## MELTING MOMENTS

1⅔ cups butter or margarine
1 cup confectioner's sugar
3 cups all-purpose flour
¼ cup custard powder
pinch of salt

**1** Cream butter and confectioner's sugar. Sift flour, custard powder, and salt together and add to the mixture.

**2** Knead well and shape teaspoonfuls of mixture into balls. Place on lightly greased cookie sheets and bake in a preheated oven at 350 °F for 15–20 minutes. Transfer to a wire rack to cool.

MAKES ABOUT 50

## CRUNCHIES

2 cups all-purpose flour
2 tsp baking powder
2 tsp baking soda
scant ½ tsp salt
1¾ cups rolled oats
1 cup dry unsweetened coconut
¼ cup wheat bran
2 sticks butter or 1 cup margarine
2 cups granulated sugar
2 tbsp corn syrup or honey

**1** Sift the flour, baking powder, baking soda, and salt. Add oats, coconut, and bran.

**2** In a heavy-based saucepan, melt the butter, sugar, and syrup and add it to the dry ingredients. Mix well. Press into a 6½ x 10½-inch tray bake pan.

**3** Bake in a preheated oven at 350 °F for 10 minutes. Cool and cut into squares.

MAKES ABOUT 24

### VARIATION
Substitute all-purpose flour with brown or granary flour for a crunchy bite.

### TIP
If sealed in an airtight container, dry unsweetened coconut freezes well for up to six months.

Clockwise from left: *Rich Almond Cookies, Butterscotch Cookies, Ginger Cookies.*

## GINGER COOKIES

2 sticks soft butter or 1 cup margarine

1 cup superfine sugar

1 large egg

1 tbsp milk

4 tbsp corn syrup or honey

2¾ cups all-purpose flour

1 tbsp ground ginger

1 tsp baking soda

½ tsp ground cinnamon

scant ½ tsp salt

2 tbsp granulated sugar for rolling

**1** Cream the butter and superfine sugar until light and fluffy. Beat in egg, then stir in the milk and syrup.

**2** Sift the flour, ginger, baking soda, cinnamon, and salt together and add to butter mixture. Mix well. Shape the dough into balls and roll them in the granulated sugar.

**3** Arrange cookies on greased cookie sheets, leaving room for spreading, and flatten slightly with a fork.

**4** Bake in a preheated oven at 350 °F for 8–10 minutes. Leave to cool slightly before transferring to a wire rack to cool completely. Store in an airtight container.

MAKES ABOUT 40

### TIP
Dip the fork in flour to minimize sticking when flattening out the cookies on a cookie sheet.

## SURPRISE BITES

1 stick butter or ½ cup margarine

¼ cup superfine sugar

1½ cups all-purpose flour

¼ cup chocolate chips

⅓ cup red candied cherries, coarsely chopped

**1** Cream butter and sugar well. Sift flour and mix well into butter mixture. Roll out dough to a thickness of about ⅛ inch. Stamp out with a round cookie cutter of about 2½ inches in diameter.

**2** Alternating between the two, place chocolate chips and cherries in the center of half of the pastry rounds. Top each with a second round of pastry and seal the edges.

**3** Bake in a preheated oven at 400 °F for 8–10 minutes. Transfer to a wire rack to cool.

MAKES ABOUT 15 DOUBLE COOKIES

---

### VARIATION
To make herb cookies: substitute chocolate chips and cherries with 4 tbsp chopped fresh mixed herbs, and knead into the dough.

---

### TIPS
- To seal the cookies, brush a little water or milk onto the edges of the dough before topping with a second dough round.
- If you don't have a cookie cutter, cut out the shapes using a thin-edged glass.

---

## SPICY OAT AND RAISIN COOKIES

2 sticks soft butter or 1 cup margarine

¾ cup superfine sugar

1 cup light brown sugar

2 large eggs

1 tsp vanilla extract

1½ cups all-purpose flour

1 tsp baking soda

½ tsp ground cinnamon

scant ½ tsp salt

1½ cups rolled oats

scant 1 cup seedless raisins

**1** Cream butter and both sugars until well mixed. Beat in eggs, one at a time, until light and fluffy. Add vanilla extract.

**2** Sift the flour, baking soda, cinnamon, and salt together. Gradually beat into butter mixture. Stir in oats and raisins. Drop teaspoonfuls of mixture onto greased cookie sheets, or shape into balls if preferred.

**3** Bake in a preheated oven at 350 °F for 8–10 minutes or until golden brown. Transfer to a wire rack to cool.

MAKES ABOUT 40

---

### TIP
Allow enough space between cookies on the cookie sheet as the dough will spread slightly.

---

## TRADITIONAL SHORTBREAD

1¼ sticks butter, softened

¾ cup superfine sugar

2¾ cups all-purpose flour

¼ cup cornstarch

scant ½ tsp salt

extra superfine sugar for sprinkling

**1** Beat butter and sugar until light and fluffy. Sift the remaining ingredients and add.

**2** Knead lightly and press into a greased 6½ x 10½-inch tray bake pan. Prick very well and bake in a preheated oven at 270 °F for about 1 hour.

**3** Cut into fingers while still hot and sprinkle with extra superfine sugar.

MAKES ABOUT 24 FINGERS

---

### VARIATION
For a citrus flavor, add 1 tbsp grated lemon or orange rind.

---

### TIP
Shortbread bakes more evenly when pricked all over with a fork.

Left to right: *Traditional Shortbread, Surprise Bites.*

## CHEESY BARBECUE COOKIES

1 cup all-purpose flour
scant 2 cups grated Cheddar cheese
3¾ stick butter or ½ cup margarine
4½-oz package barbecue flavor
potato chips, crushed

**1** Mix all ingredients together to form a soft dough.

**2** Shape teaspoonfuls of dough into balls. Place on greased cookie sheets and flatten slightly with a fork.

**3** Bake in a preheated oven at 400 °F for about 10 minutes, or until light brown. Transfer to a wire rack to cool. Store these cookies in an airtight container.

MAKES ABOUT 24

---

### VARIATION
Substitute the potato chips with any other flavor, such as cheese and onion.

---

## SPICY COOKIES

2 sticks butter
2¼ cups superfine sugar
2 large eggs
5½ cups all-purpose flour
4 tsp baking powder
2 tsp pumpkin pie spice
4 tsp ground cinnamon
1 tsp ground ginger
½ tsp ground cloves
½ tsp baking soda

**1** Cream butter and sugar. Add eggs and beat well until light and creamy.

**2** Sift remaining ingredients and add to butter mixture, with a little water if required, and bind into a dough.

**3** Roll out to a thickness of about ⅛ inch and cut out with a cookie cutter. Place on a greased cookie sheet and bake in a preheated oven at 350 °F for 8–10 minutes. Place on a rack to cool.

MAKES ABOUT 55

---

## RICH CHOCOLATE CHIP COOKIES

1 stick butter or ½ cup margarine
2 tbsp superfine sugar
½ cup condensed milk
1½ cups self-rising flour
¾ cup chocolate chips

**1** Cream butter and sugar. Beat in condensed milk, then sift flour and add to mixture with chocolate chips.

**2** Roll teaspoonfuls of mixture into balls and place on greased cookie sheets. Flatten slightly with a fork.

**3** Bake in a preheated oven at 325 °F for 15–20 minutes. Transfer to a wire rack to cool.

MAKES ABOUT 28

---

### TIP
The dough can be made in advance and refrigerated. Bake batches of cookies as required.

---

## MILLIONAIRE'S SHORTBREAD

SHORTBREAD
1 stick butter
½ cup superfine sugar
1 cup all-purpose flour
2 tbsp cornstarch
scant ½ tsp salt

FUDGE LAYER
½ stick butter
¼ cup corn syrup
1¾ cups condensed milk
½ cup superfine sugar

CHOCOLATE TOPPING
5½ oz semisweet chocolate

**1** For shortbread: beat butter and sugar until light and fluffy. Sift flour, cornstarch, and salt. Mix into butter-sugar mixture until a stiff dough is formed.

**2** Press into a greased 8 x 10-inch rectangular pan. Prick with a fork and bake in a preheated oven at 350 °F for 10 minutes. Reduce heat to 325 °F and bake for a further 10 minutes.

**3** For fudge layer: boil all ingredients in a saucepan for about 5 minutes, until thick. Beat constantly to prevent burning. Spread over baked shortbread and let cool until set.

**4** For chocolate topping: melt the chocolate in a double boiler over hot water and spread over fudge layer. Cut shortbread into squares just before chocolate hardens.

MAKES ABOUT 50

Clockwise from bottom left: *Rich Chocolate Chip Cookies, Cheesy Barbecue Cookies, Spicy Cookies, Millionaire's Shortbread.*

## RUSKS

Rusks can be made with all-purpose flour, whole-wheat flour, or a mixture of the two. Butter gives a better flavor, but if you want to store the rusks for longer, use margarine.

Dry out rusks overnight in the oven at its lowest setting (about 120 °F). Use a spoon to keep the oven door ajar so moisture can escape. Let rusks cool completely before storing (for up to three months) in an airtight container.

## GRANOLA RUSKS

3 cups butter or margarine
generous 3 cups buttermilk
2 cups superfine sugar
4 large eggs, beaten
12 cups self-rising flour
3 tbsp baking powder
1½ tsp salt
2½ cups All-Bran flakes
2½ cups granola

**1** Melt butter in a heavy-based saucepan. Add buttermilk and sugar. Remove from heat and add eggs.

**2** Sift flour, baking powder, and salt into a large bowl. Add All-Bran flakes, granola and butter mixture. Mix well.

**3** Shape into balls and pack into two large, greased roasting pans. Bake in a preheated oven at 350 °F for 45 minutes. Turn onto a rack to cool slightly; break up while still warm. Dry out overnight in the oven on its lowest setting.

MAKES ABOUT 140, DEPENDING ON SIZE

## LIGHT BRAN RUSKS

7¾ cups self-rising flour
1 tsp salt
¼ cup wheat bran
2 sticks butter or 1 cup margarine
2 large eggs
½ cup superfine sugar
2¼ cups buttermilk

**1** Sift flour and salt. Add bran. Rub in butter until mixture resembles bread crumbs. Beat eggs, sugar, and buttermilk together. Add liquid mixture to dry mixture. Mix well.

**2** Shape into balls and pack into a large, greased roasting pan.

**3** Bake in a preheated oven at 350 °F for about 50 minutes. Turn out onto a wire rack to cool slightly. Break up while still warm, and let cool further. Dry out overnight in the oven on its lowest setting.

MAKES ABOUT 50, DEPENDING ON SIZE

## BUTTERMILK-COCONUT RUSKS

12 cups self-rising flour
1 tsp salt
3 cups superfine sugar
1½ cups dry unsweetened coconut
2 tbsp aniseed (optional)
1½ cups butter or margarine
3 large eggs
2¼ cups buttermilk

**1** Sift flour. Add salt, sugar, coconut, and aniseed and rub in butter. Add eggs and buttermilk. Mix well and roll into balls. Pack into greased roasting pans.

**2** Bake in a preheated oven at 350 °F for 45 minutes until golden brown.

**3** Turn onto a rack to cool slightly; break up while still warm. Dry out overnight in the oven on its lowest setting.

MAKES ABOUT 80, DEPENDING ON SIZE

## BUTTERMILK RUSKS

16 cups self-rising flour
2 tsp salt
1 tbsp baking powder
3¼ cups butter or margarine
2 cups superfine caster sugar
2 tbsp aniseed (optional)
scant 4½ cups buttermilk
3 large eggs

**1** Sift flour, salt, and baking powder. Rub in butter until mixture resembles bread crumbs. Add sugar and aniseed.

**2** Mix buttermilk and eggs together. Add to dry ingredients and mix well.

**3** Shape into balls and pack into large, greased roasting pans. Bake in a preheated oven at 350 °F for 50–60 minutes.

**4** Turn onto a rack to cool slightly; break up while still warm. Dry out overnight in the oven on its lowest setting.

MAKES ABOUT 140, DEPENDING ON SIZE

Left to right: *Light Bran Rusks, Butternut Rusks, Granola Rusks.*

# BUTTERNUT RUSKS

generous 3 cups boiling water
1½ cups superfine sugar
1½ cups butter or margarine
3 large eggs, beaten
7¾ cups whole-wheat or
brown flour
8 tsp baking powder
2 tsp salt
1 tsp cream of tartar
¾ cup cooked, mashed
butternut squash

**1** Combine boiling water, sugar, and butter and stir until sugar has melted. Let mixture cool then add eggs.

**2** Sift flour, baking powder, salt, and cream of tartar together and add to egg mixture. Add bran from sifter and mix well. (The mixture will be runny.)

**3** Add mashed squash and mix well.

**4** Pour into three greased 9-inch loaf pans. Bake in a preheated oven at 350 °F for about 1 hour.

**5** Leave in pans for a few minutes to cool, then turn out onto a wire rack to cool completely. Cut each loaf into thick slices and divide each slice into three again.

**6** Dry out overnight in the oven at its lowest setting.

MAKES ABOUT 70, DEPENDING ON SIZE

## TIPS
- Use an electric knife to slice the rusks to prevent breakage.
- Instead of drying them out in the oven, let the rusks stand on a wire rack overnight and cut the next day. They won't break up and crumble as much.

# BARS, SQUARES, AND SWEET TREATS

*These recipes, a cross between a cookie and a cake, are ideal when you want to indulge in something small and snacky. They are mostly baked in trays and then cut into slices or squares. Storing and freezing rules are the same as for cakes.*

## CHERRY DREAM BARS

¹/₃ cup soft butter or margarine
scant ¹/₂ cup light brown sugar
1 cup all-purpose flour

TOPPING
2 large eggs
scant 1¹/₂ cups light brown sugar
¹/₄ cup all-purpose flour
¹/₂ tsp baking powder
1¹/₂ cups dry unsweetened coconut
¹/₃ cup red candied cherries, halved
1 tsp vanilla extract

**1** Cream butter and sugar. Sift flour and add. Press mixture into a greased 8-inch square baking pan. Bake in a preheated oven at 350 °F for 12 minutes. Set aside.

**2** For topping: beat eggs and sugar together. Sift flour and baking powder and add to egg mixture with all the remaining ingredients. Mix thoroughly.

**3** Spread this mixture over the warm cake and bake for 15–20 minutes until light brown. Cut into squares. Cool in the pan for a few minutes before transferring to a rack to cool further.

MAKES ABOUT 18

### VARIATION
Substitute cherries with 75 g
¹/₂ cup chopped walnuts.

## CHOCOLATE-NUT SQUARES

1 stick butter
1 cup light brown sugar
1 large egg
1 tsp vanilla extract
1 cup all-purpose flour
1 tsp baking powder
scant ¹/₂ tsp salt
scant ¹/₂ cup dry unsweetened coconut
scant ¹/₂ cup coarsely chopped pecans or walnuts
1³/₄ cups chocolate chips

TOPPING
2 tbsp chopped pecans

**1** Cream butter and sugar. Add egg and vanilla extract and beat until light and fluffy.

**2** Sift the flour, baking powder, and salt. Add it to the mixture along with the coconut, nuts, and chocolate chips. Mix well.

**3** Spoon mixture into a greased 6¹/₂ x 10¹/₂-inch tray bake pan. Sprinkle extra nuts on top.

**4** Bake in a preheated oven at 350 °F for about 25 minutes and cut into squares.

MAKES ABOUT 24

## BUTTERHORNS

2 sticks soft butter or 1 cup margarine
1¹/₂ cups sieved cottage cheese
2 cups all-purpose flour
scant ¹/₂ tsp salt

FROSTING
scant 1 cup confectioner's sugar
2 tbsp milk

**1** Cream butter and cottage cheese. Sift flour and salt and mix into the butter mixture. Refrigerate for at least 4 hours, or overnight. Divide into four pieces and roll each piece out to a thickness of ¹/₈ inch.

**2** Cut into wedges (about 5¹/₂ inches long) and roll each wedge, starting at the wide end (about 4¹/₂ inches wide) to pointed end. Place on greased baking trays. Bake in a preheated oven at 375 °F for 12–15 minutes.

**3** For frosting: mix confectioner's sugar and milk. Drizzle frosting over butterhorns while still warm.

MAKES ABOUT 22

### TIP
When creaming butter for baking, rinse the bowl with boiling water to make the task a lot easier.

Cherry Dream Bars

## GRANOLA BARS

1 ½ sticks butter or ¾ cup margarine
scant ½ cup honey or corn syrup
1 cup superfine sugar
1 ½ cups rolled oats
scant 1 cup all-purpose flour
1 tsp ground cinnamon
½ cup pecans or walnuts
⅓ cup seedless raisins
½ cup dried mango, chopped
½ cup dried apricots, chopped
scant ½ cup ground almonds
(optional)
2 tbsp sesame seeds

**1** Melt butter and honey in a saucepan over low heat, then stir in the sugar.

**2** Keep the heat low until sugar has dissolved, then bring to a boil for 1–2 minutes, stirring, until thickened and smooth.

**3** Mix together all the remaining ingredients and stir into the syrup until well combined. Press into a greased 6½ x 10½-inch tray bake pan. Press down lightly.

**4** Bake in a preheated oven at 350 °F for 25–30 minutes until just beginning to brown. Let cool and cut into bars or squares.

MAKES ABOUT 18

### TIP
When honey or corn syrup has crystallized, remove the lid and place the jar in the microwave on high for about 30 seconds, then stir until it becomes smooth.

## DECADENT BROWNIES

4 ¼ oz semisweet chocolate
2 sticks butter or 1 cup margarine
3 large eggs
generous 1 cup superfine sugar
1 tsp vanilla extract
½ cup self-rising flour
2 tbsp unsweetened cocoa
scant ½ tsp salt
½ cup chopped walnuts (optional)

**1** Melt chocolate and butter in a saucepan, then set aside to cool slightly.

**2** Beat eggs and sugar until light and fluffy. Add vanilla extract and gradually beat in the melted mixture.

**3** Sift the flour, cocoa, and salt over the mixture, then fold it in together with the walnuts (if using).

**4** Turn the mixture into a greased 6½ x 10½-inch tray bake pan. Bake in a preheated oven at 375 °F for 20–25 minutes or until just firm in the center.

**5** Let cool in the pan for a few minutes, then cut into squares and turn out onto a wire rack to cool.

MAKES ABOUT 28

### TIP
When baking brownies, be careful not to overbake them. When you insert a skewer into the center, a tiny amount of moist mixture should adhere to it, otherwise the texture will be too dry.

## GINGER SQUARES

⅓ cup butter or margarine
6 tbsp honey
scant ½ cup light brown sugar
scant ½ cup milk
2 large eggs
generous 1 ½ cups self-rising flour
1 tbsp ground ginger
scant ½ tsp baking soda

### FROSTING
½ stick butter or ¼ cup margarine
¾ cup light brown sugar
2 tbsp milk
¾ cup confectioner's sugar

**1** Place butter, honey, and sugar in a saucepan. Stir over low heat (do not boil) until sugar dissolves. Cool slightly.

**2** Stir milk, eggs, flour, ginger, and baking soda into mixture. Pour into a greased 6½ x 10½-inch tray bake pan and bake in a preheated oven at 350 °F for 25–30 minutes. Let stand for 5 minutes before turning onto a wire rack to cool.

**3** For frosting: melt butter in a small saucepan. Add brown sugar and milk, bring to a boil, then simmer, stirring, for 2 minutes. Stir in enough confectioner's sugar to make a spreadable consistency. Spread over cake and cut into squares.

MAKES 24

Clockwise from left: *Decadent Brownies, Ginger Squares, Granola Bars.*

# GRANADILLA ÉCLAIRS

½ stick butter
½ cup water
½ cup all-purpose flour
2 large eggs, lightly beaten

FILLING
1 cup heavy cream
generous ¼ cup confectioner's sugar
¾ cup granadilla or passion
fruit pulp

**1** Place butter and water in a saucepan and heat until melted. Bring to a boil and remove from heat. Sift flour and add. Stir well with a wooden spoon until the mixture forms a ball in the center of the saucepan. Let cool slightly. Add eggs, one at a time, beating well after each addition, until the dough is smooth.

**2** Pipe onto a greased cookie sheet and bake in a preheated oven at 400 °F for 18–20 minutes until puffed and golden. Remove and cut a slit in the side to let steam escape. Return to oven for 2 minutes to dry out. Transfer to a wire rack to cool.

**3** For filling: whip cream until stiff and add sugar and fruit pulp. Spoon or pipe the filling into the éclairs. Dust with extra confectioner's sugar.

MAKES ABOUT 12

## VARIATION
Fill with whipped cream and top with chocolate frosting – 1¾ oz chocolate, melted, ½ tbsp butter, 1½ cups confectioner's sugar.

# STICKY CARAMEL APPLE PIECES

3 medium Granny Smith apples

BATTER
scant 1 cup all-purpose flour
scant ½ tsp salt
1 tbsp sunflower oil
scant ½ cup warm water
2 large egg whites
oil for deep-frying

SAUCE
1 stick butter
1¼ cups soft brown sugar
½ cup heavy cream

**1** Peel and core apples and cut each one into 8–12 pieces.

**2** For batter: sift flour and salt. Add oil and water. Whisk the egg whites until soft peaks form and fold in to make a smooth batter. Mix well and let stand for 30 minutes.

**3** Coat the apple pieces in batter and deep-fry in hot oil until golden brown. Drain on paper towels.

**4** For sauce: heat butter and sugar until the sugar has dissolved. Add the cream and bring to a boil, stirring for a few minutes. Pour the sauce over apple pieces and serve immediately.

MAKES 24–36 PIECES

## VARIATION
Substitute the apples with four sliced bananas.

# TRUFFLES

3⅓ cups vanilla or chocolate
cake crumbs
½ cup pecans, chopped
½ cup dry unsweetened coconut
¼ cup superfine sugar
scant ½ tsp rum extract
¼ stick butter
5½ oz semisweet chocolate
superfine sugar, unsweetened cocoa
or melted chocolate for rolling

**1** Mix all ingredients together except butter and chocolate.

**2** Melt butter and chocolate and mix well with other ingredients. Roll teaspoonfuls of the mixture into balls and roll in sugar, cocoa, or melted chocolate.

MAKES ABOUT 30

## TIPS
- To make the truffles, use crumbs from trimmed off-cuts, flopped cakes, or even stale bits of cake.
- The secret to melting chocolate is to melt it slowly over low heat in a double boiler. Alternatively, heat at 50% power in a 750-watt microwave for 2–4 mins. (The time required depends on volume.) Stir after each minute until shiny and melted.

Clockwise from left: *Granadilla Éclairs, Sticky Caramel Apple Pieces, Truffles.*

# BRANDY SNAP ROLLS

¾ cup superfine sugar
1 stick butter
¼ cup corn syrup
1 cup all-purpose flour
1 tsp ground ginger
1 tsp fresh lemon juice
2 tbsp brandy

FILLING
½ cup heavy cream
1 tbsp superfine sugar

**1** Heat the sugar, butter, and syrup together until the sugar dissolves. Remove from heat. Sift the flour and ginger and stir it into butter mixture. Add lemon juice and brandy and stir until smooth.

**2** Place heaping teaspoonfuls well apart on greased cookie sheets.

**3** Bake in a preheated oven at 325 °F for 8–10 minutes until golden brown. Remove from oven and leave for a few seconds to cool.

**4** As soon as you're able to handle the snaps, roll them around the handles of greased wooden spoons.

**5** For filling: whip cream and sugar until stiff and pipe into or fill rolls.

MAKES ABOUT 20

## VARIATION
Create baskets by pressing the snaps over oranges or something round. Fill with fresh fruit, berries, and cream or custard.

# CHEWY APRICOT BARS

1 cup self-rising flour
1 tsp ground cinnamon
scant ½ tsp salt
4 tbsp wheat bran
½ cup light brown sugar
½ cup dried apricots, chopped
½ cup chopped walnuts or pecans
6 tbsp corn syrup or honey
2 tbsp milk

**1** Sift flour, cinnamon, and salt together. Add bran.

**2** Add sugar, apricots, and nuts. Add syrup and milk and mix well.

**3** Spread the mixture in a greased 8-inch square cake pan and bake in a preheated oven at 350 °F for 20–25 minutes. Remove from oven and cut into bars or squares.

MAKES ABOUT 15

# CHOCOLATE-COCONUT SLICES

2 sticks butter or 1 cup margarine
½ cup superfine sugar
2 cups all-purpose flour
3 tbsp unsweetened cocoa
2¼ cups dry unsweetened coconut

TOPPING
1 stick butter or ½ cup margarine
1¾ cups confectioner's sugar
½ cup unsweetened cocoa
1 tbsp milk

**1** Cream butter and sugar. Sift the flour and cocoa, add coconut, and mix it all into the butter mixture.

**2** Press into a greased 9 x 13-inch jelly roll pan

**3** Bake in a preheated oven at 350 °F for 20–25 minutes.

**4** For topping: melt butter in a heavy-based saucepan and add confectioner's sugar and cocoa. Add milk and mix well. Remove from heat and spread over base while still warm. Cut into slices.

MAKES ABOUT 40

# CHERRY BALLS

scant 1 cup self-rising flour
¼ cup butter or margarine
generous ¼ cup superfine sugar
1 large egg, beaten
1 tbsp milk
about 15 candied cherries
oil for deep-frying
generous 1 cup superfine sugar
for rolling

**1** Sift the flour and rub in butter. Add sugar.

**2** Add beaten egg and milk to flour and mix to a soft dough.

**3** Form balls of dough with cherries inside. Deep-fry in hot oil until golden brown and drain on paper towels. Roll in superfine sugar.

MAKES ABOUT 15

Clockwise from top left: *Chocolate-Coconut Slices, Chewy Apricot Bars, Cherry Balls.*

## KOEKSISTERS

### SYRUP

5 cups granulated sugar

2¼ cups water

2 pieces gingerroot, slightly bruised

pinch of cream of tartar

pinch of salt

1 tsp grated lemon rind

½ cup fresh lemon juice

### DOUGH

2 cups all-purpose flour

4 tsp baking powder

½ tsp salt

¼ stick butter

½ cup buttermilk or water with
lemon juice

oil for deep-frying

**1** For syrup: place all ingredients in a saucepan and stir over low heat until the sugar has dissolved. Cover and boil for a few minutes. Do not stir. Remove from heat and chill.

**2** For dough: sift the dry ingredients together and rub in the butter until mixture resembles bread crumbs.

**3** Add the liquid and mix to a soft dough. Knead until smooth.

**4** Cover and let stand for about 15 minutes. Roll to a thickness of ¼ inch and cut into strips of 2 inches in width and scant 3 inches in length. Starting ½ inch from the top, cut each strip into three.

**5** Plait together three strips at a time and press the ends firmly together.

**6** Deep-fry in hot oil until golden and well-done. Drain on paper towels and dip into ice-cold syrup.

MAKES ABOUT 24

### TIPS

- To check if oil is hot enough for frying, dip a cube of bread into the oil – it should turn brown within 90 seconds.
- Koeksisters freeze successfully in an airtight container. Remove from the freezer 30 minutes before serving.

# QUICK LOAVES AND LARGE CAKES

*The aroma from the oven and the taste of freshly baked cakes still make all of us appreciate Mom! Round cake pans are still the most widely used for cakes, but square pans, loaf pans and large rectangular pans are popular too. The cake mixture should only reach to half to two-thirds of the pan, leaving enough space for the cake to rise. For successful cakes, use only the best ingredients at room temperature, and weigh and measure accurately. Also take care with the lining and greasing of the pans.*

## WHISKING

Place eggs and sugar in a large bowl and whisk until light and thick. If not using an electric mixer, set the bowl over a saucepan of hot water. Sponges made using this method are very light in texture.

## CREAMING

Preferably use an electric mixer, as vigorous beating will be required when mixing by hand or with a wooden spoon. Beat soft butter and sugar together until light and creamy – it should have a very smooth consistency. Beat the eggs into the creamed mixture, one at a time, beating well after each addition. To prevent curdling, add a little flour to the eggs.

## FOLDING IN

Sift the flour over the creamed or whisked cake mixture, holding the sifter above the mixture to let it fall and aerate. Use a large metal spoon or whisk, cutting and carefully folding the flour into the mixture using a figure of eight movement.

## LINING TINS

For sponges, place pan on waxed paper, draw around it and cut out 2 inches wider around the base. Snip the lining at intervals. Lining for sides should be placed first, then the base. Grease the pan as well as the paper. Special baking parchment can also be used. Even nonstick pans need greasing, and this can be done by brushing on butter or spraying the pan with nonstick spray. Flour can also be dusted on to prevent sticking.

## TESTING GUIDELINES

– When a sponge pulls away from the sides of the pan, it is done.
– A quick loaf is baked when the top looks and feels firm and dry.
– A cake is ready when a cake tester inserted into the center comes out dry. If the center is still raw, return to the oven for a further 5–8 minutes.
– Loaves with a soft, cakelike texture can be left to stand for 10 minutes to firm up slightly before being turned out onto a wire rack to cool.

## STORING

Cakes should be cooled to room temperature before storing in an airtight container. Quick loaves and unfrosted cakes keep well for up to three months if frozen in airtight freezer wrap or bags. Leave the loaves to thaw at room temperature before serving. If frosting is not used, dust confectioner's sugar over the top for an appealing finish before serving. Freeze whisked sponges for up to one month only. Cakes such as Madeira keep well for up to four days if sealed tightly. Fruit cakes and gingerbread actually improve with age. Most cakes, however, are enjoyed freshly baked.

## FROSTING

Frosting adds color and flavor to cakes and prevents them from drying out. Only frost cakes once completely cool.

Some frostings are spread over the cake, others are poured over. Do not overmix the frosting as it will become runny. Use a round-bladed knife dipped in hot water for easy spreading. For a textured effect, draw the knife forward and backward across the cake. Once a cake has been frosted, the sides can be coated with grated chocolate or chopped or flaked nuts.

## BUTTER FROSTING

¾ stick soft butter
1½ cups confectioner's sugar
2 tsp vanilla extract
about 5 tsp milk

**1** Cream butter, sugar and vanilla extract. Add enough milk to make mixture light and creamy, and of a spreadable consistency.

**2** Sandwich the layers of cake together with frosting then frost the top.

---

### VARIATION

Omit vanilla extract and add grated citrus rind, fresh citrus juice, sieved cottage cheese, unsweetened cocoa, or coffee powder.

---

Meringue Cake (page 44)

## PINEAPPLE CAKE

### CAKE
1 stick butter or ½ cup margarine
generous 1 cup superfine sugar
2 large eggs
3¼ cups self-rising flour
⅓ cup milk

### FILLING
14-oz can crushed pineapple
1 cup superfine sugar
2 large eggs, lightly beaten
¼ cup custard powder

**1** For cake: cream the butter and sugar. Add eggs and beat until light and fluffy.

**2** Sift flour and add, alternately with milk, to egg mixture. Divide between four lined and greased 9-inch cake pans. Level with a round-bladed knife.

**3** Bake in a preheated oven at 350 °F for about 20 minutes until light brown. Let cool slightly in the pan, then turn out onto a wire rack to cool.

**4** For filling: boil pineapple, sugar, and eggs for 3 minutes, stirring constantly.

**5** Mix custard powder with a little cold water and stir into pineapple mixture. Boil until thick. Let cool.

**6** Spread filling over three of the cakes and stack them on top of each other. Crumble the remaining cake and spread over the top. Store in an airtight container for 24 hours before serving.

MAKES 1 LARGE CAKE

## MADEIRA COCONUT LOAF

1 stick butter
generous ½ cup superfine sugar
3 large egg yolks
1 tsp vanilla extract
1 cup all-purpose flour
2 tsp baking powder
pinch of salt
½ cup milk

### TOPPING
3 large egg whites
⅔ cup superfine sugar
¾ cup dry unsweetened coconut

**1** Cream butter and sugar. Add egg yolks, one at a time, beating well after each addition, until light and fluffy. Add vanilla extract.

**2** Sift flour, baking powder, and salt and add, alternately with milk, to butter mixture.

**3** Spoon the mixture into a greased 9-inch loaf pan.

**4** For topping: whisk egg whites until stiff. Add sugar and beat well. Add coconut and mix. Spoon on top of cake mixture.

**5** Bake in a preheated oven at 350 °F for 30 minutes. Reduce temperature to 325 °F and bake for another 15–20 minutes. Carefully turn out onto a wire rack to cool.

MAKES 1 LOAF

## BANANA LOAF

1 stick butter or ½ cup margarine
1 cup superfine sugar
2 large eggs
1 tsp vanilla extract
2 cups all-purpose flour
1 tsp baking powder
pinch of salt
1 tsp baking soda
3–4 mashed ripe bananas
2 tbsp fresh lemon juice

**1** Cream butter and sugar. Add eggs, one at a time, beating well after each addition. Add vanilla extract.

**2** Sift dry ingredients and mix into butter mixture along with mashed banana and lemon juice.

**3** Spoon into a greased 9-inch loaf pan. Bake in a preheated oven at 350 °F, for 1 hour. Turn out onto a wire rack to cool.

MAKES 1 LOAF

### VARIATIONS
Substitute half all-purpose flour with whole-wheat flour and add ½ cup chopped pecans or walnuts.
Substitute vanilla extract with almond extract.

Clockwise from top left: *Madeira Coconut Loaf, Banana Loaf, Pineapple Cake.*

## APRICOT JELLY ROLL

4 large eggs

3 tbsp apricot juice

1 cup superfine sugar

1 cup all-purpose flour

2 tsp baking powder

pinch of salt

superfine sugar for rolling

about $\frac{1}{2}$ cup smooth apricot jelly

**1** Beat eggs until light and fluffy, then beat in apricot juice. Add sugar gradually and beat until dissolved.

**2** Sift the dry ingredients in thin layers over the egg mixture and fold in lightly with a spatula. Repeat until all the dry ingredients have been used. Spoon the mixture into a greased and lined 9 x 13-inch jelly roll pan.

**3** Bake in a preheated oven at 400 °F for 10–12 minutes. Turn onto a clean, dry dish towel sprinkled with superfine sugar. Trim edges to ensure rolling without breaking.

**4** Spread a thin layer of apricot jelly over the cake. Roll up and wrap in the towel. Leave for a minute or two, then remove towel and let cool.

MAKES 1 CAKE

### VARIATION
Chocolate roll: Substitute 4 tbsp flour with 3 tbsp unsweetened cocoa. Use strong, black coffee instead of juice. Roll with buttered waxed paper, cool, and fill with whipped cream. Roll up.

## ORANGE AND ZUCCHINI LOAF

$\frac{1}{2}$ cup superfine sugar

$\frac{1}{2}$ cup sunflower oil or melted butter

1 large egg

1 tsp vanilla extract

2 cups self-rising flour

scant $\frac{1}{2}$ tsp baking soda

1 tsp ground cinnamon

scant $\frac{1}{2}$ tsp salt

pinch of grated nutmeg

pinch of ground cloves

4 tbsp wheat bran

1 tbsp grated orange rind

$\frac{1}{2}$ cup fresh orange juice

1 cup grated zucchini

$\frac{1}{2}$ cup chopped walnuts

$\frac{1}{2}$ cup seedless raisins

**1** Beat sugar, oil, and egg until light and fluffy. Add vanilla extract. Sift all dry ingredients and add to mixture, with bran.

**2** Add remaining ingredients and mix well. Spoon into a greased 9-inch loaf pan.

**3** Bake in a preheated oven at 350 °F for 35–45 minutes. Turn out onto a wire rack to cool.

MAKES 1 LOAF

### TIP
To make vanilla sugar, pour some superfine sugar into a clean jar and add a vanilla bean. Store in a cool, dark place for about a week to allow the flavor to develop.

## SOUR CREAM CINNAMON CAKE

1 cup sour cream

1 tsp baking soda

1 stick butter or $\frac{1}{2}$ cup margarine

$\frac{1}{2}$ cup superfine caster sugar

2 large eggs

1 tsp vanilla extract

2 cups all-purpose flour

2 tsp baking powder

TOPPING

scant $\frac{1}{2}$ cup raw brown sugar

1 tsp ground cinnamon

$\frac{1}{4}$ cup pecan nuts, chopped

**1** Mix sour cream and baking soda in a bowl. Set aside.

**2** Cream butter and sugar. Add eggs and vanilla extract and beat well until light and fluffy.

**3** Sift dry ingredients. Add to butter mixture, with the sour cream. Spoon half the mixture into a greased 9-inch loose-bottomed round cake pan.

**4** For topping: mix all ingredients together. Sprinkle half the topping mixture over the cake. Cover with remaining mixture, then sprinkle over remainder of the topping. Bake in a preheated oven at 350 °F for 35–45 minutes. Serve warm or cold.

MAKES 1 CAKE

### TIP
This delicious cake will stay moist for up to two days.

Left to right: *Sour Cream Cinnamon Cake, Orange and Zucchini Loaf.*

## POPPY SEED DELIGHT

3 large eggs
1 cup superfine sugar
$\frac{1}{2}$ cup sunflower oil or melted
butter
1 cup self-rising flour
$\frac{3}{4}$ cup plain yogurt
$\frac{3}{4}$ cup dry unsweetened coconut
4 tbsp poppy seeds

### LEMON FROSTING
$\frac{1}{4}$ stick soft butter
1$\frac{1}{2}$ cups confectioner's sugar
1 tsp grated lemon rind
2–3 tbsp fresh lemon juice

**1** Beat the eggs and sugar until light and fluffy.

**2** Add oil and beat well. Sift flour and add, along with the yogurt, coconut and poppy seeds.

**3** Pour into a greased 9$\frac{1}{2}$-inch square cake pan or ovenproof dish. Bake in a preheated oven at 350 °F for 35–40 minutes. Let cool in the pan.

**4** For frosting: cream butter, confectioner's sugar, and rind. Add enough juice to mixture to make it light and creamy, and of a spreadable consistency. Frost the top of the cake and cut into squares.

MAKES ABOUT 16 SQUARES

---

### TIP
When only a few drops of orange or lemon juice are required, use a thick skewer to pierce the skin in a few places and squeeze the fruit for juice to run out.

---

## BUTTERMILK CAKE

1 stick butter
1$\frac{1}{2}$ cups light brown sugar
2 large eggs
1 tsp vanilla extract
2 cups self-rising flour
scant $\frac{1}{2}$ tsp salt
1 cup buttermilk
$\frac{1}{2}$ cup currants
confectioner's sugar for dusting

**1** Cream butter and sugar. Add eggs and vanilla extract and beat well until light and fluffy.

**2** Sift flour and salt and add, alternately with buttermilk, to sugar mixture. Add currants, mixing well.

**3** Spoon into a greased 9-inch loaf pan. Bake in a preheated oven at 325 °F for 50–60 minutes.

**4** Turn out onto a wire rack to cool. Dust with confectioner's sugar.

MAKES 1 LOAF

---

## PRUNE CAKE

1 stick butter or $\frac{1}{2}$ cup margarine
1 cup superfine sugar
3 large eggs
1$\frac{1}{4}$ cups pitted prunes
2 cups all-purpose flour
1 tbsp baking powder
scant $\frac{1}{2}$ tsp baking soda
1 tsp pumpkin pie spice
1 tsp ground cinnamon
scant $\frac{1}{2}$ tsp salt
$\frac{1}{2}$ cup buttermilk
scant 1 cup apple juice

---

### CREAM CHEESE FROSTING
$\frac{3}{4}$ stick butter
2$\frac{3}{4}$ cups confectioner's sugar
$\frac{1}{2}$ cup sieved cottage cheese
1 tsp vanilla extract
chopped nuts to decorate

**1** Cream butter and sugar. Add eggs, one at a time, beating well after each addition until light and fluffy. Chop the prunes as fine as possible and add.

**2** Sift dry ingredients together and add, alternately with buttermilk and apple juice, to egg mixture.

**3** Pour into two greased 8-inch round cake pans. Bake in a preheated oven at 350 °F for 30–35 minutes. Cool on a rack.

**4** For frosting: cream butter, then add sugar and remaining ingredients. Mix until blended; do not overmix as it will become runny. Frost the cooled cake and decorate with chopped nuts.

MAKES 1 LARGE CAKE

---

### VARIATION
Substitute cottage cheese with mashed banana for an alternative delicious frosting.

Left to right: *Sweet Potato Loaf, Poppy Seed Delight, Prune Cake.*

## SWEET POTATO LOAF

2 sticks butter or 1 cup
margarine
¾ cup brown sugar
2 large eggs
¼ cup corn syrup or honey
2 cups self-rising flour
1½ tsp ground ginger
1 tsp ground cinnamon
1 cup cooked, mashed
sweet potato

CARAMEL FROSTING
½ stick soft butter
generous ¼ cup brown sugar
1 cup confectioner's sugar
1 tsp caramel extract
about 5 tsp milk

**1** Cream butter and sugar. Add eggs, one at a time, beating until light and fluffy. Beat in corn syrup.

**2** Sift dry ingredients and add, with cold sweet potato, to mixture. Spoon into a greased 9-inch loaf pan.

**3** Bake in a preheated oven at 350 °F for 40–45 minutes. Leave in pan for a few minutes before cooling on wire rack.

**4** For frosting: cream butter and sugar. Add confectioner's sugar, caramel extract and enough milk to make frosting creamy. Frost the top of the loaf.

MAKES 1 LOAF

### VARIATION
Instead of frosting the cake, dust confectioner's sugar over the top.

### TIP
If frosting is too soft, cornstarch or custard powder can be added to stiffen it up if no more confectioner's sugar is available.

## BEET AND CARROT CAKE

1 cup superfine sugar

1 cup corn or sunflower oil

3 large eggs, separated

2 tsp caramel extract

2 cups all-purpose flour

pinch of salt

2 tsp baking powder

$^1/_2$ cup grated raw beets

$^1/_2$ cup grated raw carrots

4 tbsp milk

### SYRUP

$^1/_2$ cup granulated sugar

$^1/_2$ cup water

scant $^1/_2$ tsp caramel extract

**1**  Beat sugar, oil, and egg yolks. Add caramel extract.

**2**  Sift dry ingredients and beat into sugar mixture. Whisk egg whites until soft peaks form and fold into sugar mixture.

**3**  Add grated beets, carrots, and milk and mix well. Spoon mixture into a greased 9-inch loose-bottomed springform pan.

**4**  Bake in a preheated oven at 350 °F for 25–30 minutes.

**5**  For syrup: boil sugar and water until sugar dissolves. Remove from heat, add caramel extract, and pour syrup over the cake as soon as it comes out of the oven.

MAKES 1 LARGE CAKE

## LEMON LOAF

1 stick butter or $^1/_2$ cup margarine

1 cup superfine sugar

2 large eggs

1 tsp grated lemon rind

$1^1/_2$ cups all-purpose flour

2 tsp baking powder

scant $^1/_2$ tsp salt

$^1/_2$ cup milk

### TOPPING

4 tbsp granulated sugar

$^1/_2$ cup fresh lemon juice

**1**  Cream butter and sugar. Beat in eggs and rind. Sift the dry ingredients together and add, alternately with milk, to creamed mixture. Spoon into a greased 9-inch loaf pan.

**2**  Bake in a preheated oven at 350 °F for 40–45 minutes, or until done. Cool in pan.

**3**  For topping: boil sugar and lemon juice for about 3 minutes. Spoon syrup over loaf in pan while still hot. Leave cake for a few more minutes in pan before turning out onto a wire rack to cool further.

MAKES 1 LOAF

> **TIP**
> A medium lemon yields about 1 tbsp grated rind and 3 tbsp juice.

## HONEY CAKE

2 tbsp butter or margarine

scant $^1/_2$ cup superfine sugar

1 large egg

1 cup all-purpose flour

1 tbsp baking powder

$^1/_2$ cup milk

### TOPPING

$^3/_4$ stick butter

$^1/_3$ cup honey

**1**  Cream butter and sugar. Add egg and beat until light and fluffy.

**2**  Sift dry ingredients and add, with milk, to butter mixture. Mix well. Spoon mixture into a greased 9-inch round or rectangular ovenproof dish. Bake in a preheated oven at 350 °F for 20–25 minutes.

**3**  For topping: melt butter and honey in a saucepan and pour syrup over cake while still hot. Cut the cake into wedges or squares and serve.

MAKES 1 CAKE

> **TIP**
> If honey crystallizes, place the jar in warm water until liquefied.

Left to right: *Lemon Loaf, Beet and Carrot Cake.*

39

# PEANUT BUTTER LOAF

¾ cup crunchy or
smooth peanut butter
¾ stick soft butter
2 cups all-purpose flour
½ cup superfine sugar
2 tsp baking powder
scant ½ tsp salt
scant 1 cup milk
2 tsp grated orange rind
2 large eggs, beaten

**1** Mix peanut butter and butter. Sift dry ingredients and mix into peanut butter mixture. Add milk, rind, and eggs and mix well.

**2** Spoon into a greased 9-inch loaf pan. Bake in a preheated oven at 350 °F for about 50 minutes. Cool in pan for 10 minutes and transfer to a rack to cool further.

MAKES 1 LOAF

# BUTTER CAKE

1 stick butter
1 cup superfine sugar
4 large eggs, separated
1 tsp vanilla extract
2 cups all-purpose flour
2 tsp baking powder
pinch of salt
½ cup milk
⅓ cup water
1 tsp cream of tartar

### BUTTER FROSTING
1 stick butter
1½ cups confectioner's sugar
1 tsp vanilla extract
1 tbsp milk, if required

**1** Cream the butter and sugar. Add the egg yolks and beat well until light and fluffy. Add vanilla extract.

**2** Sift the dry ingredients and add, alternately with the milk and water.

**3** Whisk the egg whites with the cream of tartar until stiff. Using a large metal spoon, fold the egg whites into the flour mixture.

**4** Pour into two 8-inch round, greased and lined cake pans. Bake in a preheated oven at 350 °F for 30–35 minutes. Cool slightly in pans, then turn onto a rack.

**5** For frosting: beat all the ingredients together until smooth and creamy in consistency. Let cake cool completely and sandwich with half the frosting. Frost the top of the cake with remaining frosting.

MAKES 1 LARGE CAKE

---

## VARIATIONS

Passion fruit cake: Add 2 tbsp passion fruit pulp to cake mixture and 2 tbsp to the frosting.
Orange cake: Substitute milk and water with orange juice. Omit the vanilla extract and add 1 tsp grated orange rind.
Nut cake: Add ½ cup chopped walnuts to mixture.
Spice cake: Sift 1 tsp ground cinnamon, 1 tsp ground ginger and scant ½ tsp ground cloves with dry ingredients. Omit vanilla.
Chocolate cake: Mix ¼ cup unsweetened cocoa with 3 tbsp lukewarm milk and add to mixture.

---

# CARROT CAKE

scant 1 cup corn or sunflower oil
1½ cups light brown sugar
1½ cups all-purpose flour
1½ tsp baking powder
½ tsp baking soda
2 tsp ground cinnamon
1 tsp ground ginger
scant ½ tsp salt
3 large eggs, beaten
1¼ cups grated carrots
½ cup chopped pecans (optional)

### CREAM CHEESE FROSTING
½ stick butter or ¼ cup margarine, softened
generous 2 cups confectioner's sugar
1 tsp vanilla extract
½ cup sieved cottage cheese

**1** Beat together oil and sugar. Sift dry ingredients and add half to oil-sugar mixture. Mix well. Add remaining dry ingredients, alternately with eggs.

**2** Add carrots and nuts (if using) and mix well. Spoon into a greased 9-inch loose-bottomed round pan or a 8¾-inch ring pan.

**3** Bake in a preheated oven at 350 °F for 50–60 minutes. Let cool slightly in pan before turning onto a rack to cool completely.

**4** For frosting: cream butter, then add confectioner's sugar and remaining ingredients. Mix until blended; do not overmix as it will become runny. Spread on top of cake and decorate with extra chopped nuts if desired.

MAKES 1 LARGE CAKE

Clockwise from top left: *Peanut Butter Loaf, Carrot Cake, Butter Cake.*

## MOIST DARK CHOCOLATE CAKE

1 stick butter

1 cup superfine sugar

3 large eggs

2 tbsp smooth apricot jelly

1 cup boiling water

2 tsp instant coffee powder

2 cups all-purpose flour

3 tbsp unsweetened cocoa

1 tsp baking powder

2 tsp baking soda

pinch of salt

### BUTTER FROSTING

1 stick butter

1½ cups confectioner's sugar

3 tbsp unsweetened cocoa

1 tsp vanilla extract

1 tbsp milk, if required

**1** Cream butter and sugar. Add eggs, one at a time, beating well after each addition until light and fluffy. Add apricot jelly.

**2** Add boiling water to coffee powder and leave to cool slightly.

**3** Sift dry ingredients and add, alternately with coffee, to egg mixture. Turn into two lined, greased 8-inch round cake pans. Bake in a preheated oven at 350 °F for 20–25 minutes. Cool slightly in pans before turning out onto a rack.

**4** For frosting: beat all the ingredients until smooth and creamy. Sandwich cakes with half the frosting, then frost the top with the remainder.

MAKES 1 LARGE CAKE

# ULTIMATE CHEESECAKE

### PASTRY
1 cup all-purpose flour
scant 1/2 tsp baking powder
3 tbsp superfine sugar
1/2 stick butter or 1/4 cup margarine
1 tsp grated lemon rind
scant 1/2 tsp vanilla extract
1 large egg yolk

### FILLING
4 cups sieved cottage cheese
1 cup sour cream
3/4 cup superfine sugar
1/4 cup all-purpose flour
3 large eggs
1 tsp vanilla extract
1 tsp grated lemon rind

### TOPPING
1 cup granadilla or passion
fruit pulp
2 tbsp superfine sugar
4 tbsp orange juice
about 1 tbsp cornstarch

**1** For pastry: sift flour and baking powder. Add sugar. Rub in butter with your fingertips until crumbly. Add lemon rind, extract and egg yolk. Knead lightly on floured counter. Refrigerate for at least 30 minutes.

**2** Press pastry onto base and sides of a greased 9-inch round springform pan. Bake in a preheated oven at 400 °F for about 8 minutes. Remove from oven and cool. Reduce oven temperature to 325 °F.

**3** For filling: beat together the cottage cheese, sour cream, sugar, and flour until smooth.

**4** Add eggs, one at a time, vanilla extract and lemon rind and mix well. Pour the filling into the pie shell and bake for 1–1 1/4 hours, or until set. Remove from the oven.

**5** For topping: combine all the ingredients in a saucepan and heat until thickened. Pour topping over filling, cool, and refrigerate to set.

MAKES 1 LARGE CAKE

---

### VARIATION
Divide filling in half and add 1/4 cup unsweetened cocoa to one half. Spoon the chocolate mix on top of the cheesecake before baking or swirl through.

---

### TIP
When cheesecakes are difficult to cut, use a thin-bladed knife that has been moistened with a warm, wet towel. Push the blade lengthwise into the cake and pull it straight out from the bottom. Clean and moisten the blade with the wet towel before each cut.

---

# APRICOT-ALMOND CAKE

### BASE
1/2 stick butter or 1/4 cup margarine
1/2 cup superfine sugar
1 large egg
1 1/4 cups self-rising flour

### TOPPING
1/2 cup smooth apricot jelly
14-oz can apricot halves
in syrup
3/4 stick butter
3/4 cup superfine sugar
2 large eggs
1/3 cup self-rising flour
scant 1/2 cup ground almonds
2 tbsp reserved apricot syrup
scant 1/2 tsp almond extract
confectioner's sugar for dusting

**1** For base: cream butter and sugar. Add egg and beat until light and fluffy.

**2** Sift flour. Mix into sugar mixture. Knead lightly. Press into a 9 x 13-inch greased jelly roll pan.

**3** For topping: spread jelly over base. Drain apricots, but reserve liquid. Place apricots on jelly, round sides up.

**4** Cream butter and superfine sugar. Add eggs, one at a time, beating well until light and fluffy.

**5** Sift flour and add to mixture with almonds, 2 tbsp apricot syrup, and extract. Spoon over apricot halves.

**6** Bake in a preheated oven at 350 °F for 30–35 minutes. Remove from the oven and leave to cool completely in the pan. Dust with confectioner's sugar and cut into squares.

MAKES ABOUT 30 SQUARES

---

### VARIATION
Substitute apricot halves with any other canned fruit.

Clockwise from top: *Ultimate Cheesecake, Apricot-Almond Cake, Ultimate Cheesecake (Chocolate variation).*

# MOIST BUTTERMILK CHOCOLATE CAKE

1 stick butter

½ cup superfine sugar

1 tsp vanilla extract

2 large eggs

¾ cup smooth apricot jelly

1¼ cups self-rising flour

½ tsp baking soda

½ cup unsweetened cocoa

1 cup buttermilk

### CHOCOLATE FROSTING

4½ oz semisweet chocolate

½ stick butter

2 tbsp cream (optional)

**1** Cream butter and sugar. Add vanilla extract and eggs, one at a time, and beat until light and fluffy. Add jelly and beat until smooth.

**2** Sift flour, baking soda, and cocoa and add, alternately with buttermilk, to butter mixture. Mix until smooth.

**3** Line a loose-bottomed round cake pan about 8¾-inches in diameter with waxed paper and spoon in mixture. Bake in a preheated oven at 350 °F for 35–40 minutes. Let cool slightly in the pan before turning onto a wire rack to cool.

**4** For chocolate frosting: combine chocolate, butter, and cream in a saucepan and stir over low heat until smooth. Remove from heat and spread over cake.

MAKES 1 LARGE CAKE

# MERINGUE CAKE

*Serve this cake on the day of baking as it will begin to soften after it has been assembled.*

### BASE

1 stick butter or ½ cup margarine

½ cup superfine sugar

4 large egg yolks

1 cup all-purpose flour

2 tsp baking powder

scant ½ tsp salt

½ cup milk

### MERINGUE

4 large egg whites

pinch of cream of tartar

¾ cup superfine sugar

½ cup chopped pecans (optional)

### CUSTARD

1½ cups milk

2 tbsp superfine sugar

3 tbsp custard powder

1 tsp vanilla extract

½ cup heavy cream, whipped (optional)

**1** For base: cream butter and sugar.

**2** Add the egg yolks, one at a time, and beat until light and fluffy. Sift the dry ingredients together and add, alternately with the milk, to the mixture.

**3** Divide the mixture between two greased, lined 9-inch round, loose-bottomed cake pans

**4** For meringue: whisk the egg whites until foamy. Add cream of tartar and continue to whisk.

**5** Gradually whisk in the sugar until soft peaks form. Fold in the nuts. Spread the meringue over the uncooked cake mixture.

**6** Bake in a preheated oven at 325 °F for about 30 minutes, or until the meringue is golden. Let cool slightly in pans before removing to cool further.

**7** For custard: heat milk, then add sugar and custard powder, stirring until thickened. Let cool, add vanilla extract and fold in the whipped cream (if using).

**8** To assemble: place one cake layer, meringue side up, on a serving plate. Spread the custard over this layer and top with the remaining cake layer, meringue side up.

MAKES 1 LARGE CAKE

### VARIATIONS

Instead of vanilla extract, add a liqueur, such as kirsch, to the custard.

Fold whole or sliced strawberries into the cold custard and use extra strawberries to garnish.

Add 1 oz chocolate to the hot milk to make a chocolate custard.

### TIP

To whisk egg whites easily, add a few drops of fresh lemon juice.

Left to right: *Moist Buttermilk Chocolate Cake, Apple Loaf.*

## APPLE LOAF

1 stick butter or ½ cup margarine,
softened

1 cup superfine sugar

2 large eggs

1 tsp vanilla extract

2 cups all-purpose flour

scant ½ tsp salt

1 tsp baking powder

½ tsp baking soda

1 tsp ground cinnamon

scant ½ tsp grated nutmeg

½ cup milk

2 tart apples, peeled and chopped

½ cup chopped walnuts or pecans

**1** Cream butter and sugar. Add eggs, one at a time, and extract and mix.

**2** Sift together the flour, salt, baking powder, baking soda, cinnamon, and nutmeg. Gradually beat the dry ingredients, alternately with the milk, into butter mixture. Stir in apples and walnuts. Spoon into a greased 9-inch loaf pan.

**3** Bake in a preheated oven at 350 °F for 50–60 minutes. Cool for 10 minutes in the pan. Turn onto a rack to cool.

MAKES 1 LOAF

### VARIATIONS

Add scant 1 cup chocolate chips to mixture just before baking. If you do not have any fresh apples, use a 14-oz can apple pie filling instead. Alternatively, use any other fruit of choice.

# BREADS

*It is known that kneading bread is therapeutic. These days though, bread-making has become easy due to the availability of active dry yeast, which is added directly to the dry ingredients. The advantage of using active dry yeast is that the dough may need only one rising, and proving time may be reduced. The yeast can be stored in a cool, dry place for up to 18 months.*

## TYPES

Kneaded breads are made by adding enough flour to form a stiff dough that has to be kneaded, such as for rolls and pita breads. With batter breads, the ingredients are combined and beaten to make a soft, sticky dough that is not kneaded. This soft batter dough requires a container or a pan for baking.

## LIQUIDS

Yeast needs warm liquid to dissolve and activate it. The liquid should feel warm on the back of your hand, ideally around 86–95 °F. A guide, if no thermometer is available, is to add one-third boiling liquid to two-thirds cold. If the liquid is too cold, the dough will rise too slowly. If it is too hot, it will kill the yeast.

A loaf made with water will have a heavy, crisp crust and a chewy texture, like French breads. Milk, which is very popular for breads, gives a light, even texture and a thin brown crust, and adding fat keeps bread fresh for longer. Buttermilk and yogurt make a fine-textured bread with a rich flavor.

## MIXING

Mixing starts when warm liquid is stirred into dry ingredients containing yeast. This starts activating the yeast.

When mixing dough, it is important to know how bread should feel. Mixing by hand can take up to 10 minutes. All flours vary slightly in the amount of liquid they absorb. The amount of flour in a recipe is a guide. Because of atmospheric and technical influences, bread is unique with every mixing. Experience will later guide you.

## KNEADING AND PROVING

Lightly flour your hands. Gently bring the far edge of dough forward and fold it over. With the heel of your hand, push the dough away from you; give the dough a quarter turn and repeat. Keep folding and turning until the dough feels smooth. Kneading makes dough smooth and elastic. If dough starts to stick to your hands or to the surface, flour them. Add a little flour at first, as too much flour will result in a stiff, dry bread. When kneaded sufficiently, the dough should feel supple and elastic, and should spring back if pressed with a finger. If the dough is too soft, work in a little more flour.

Grease deep plastic containers by brushing with oil or using nonstick spray. Place the ball of dough in the container and turn it over to grease the other side. Plastic wrap works well as a cover to keep in the moisture. Let the dough prove in a warm place, away from drafts, until doubled in size. It is difficult to predict an exact proving time as this depends on the temperature of the dough, the amount of yeast, and general atmospheric conditions.

## PUNCHING DOWN AND SECOND PROVING

After it has risen, punch down the dough and knead briefly until the original volume is achieved. This ensures an even texture. Shape the dough – use your imagination and form your own shapes. Once a shape is formed, try not to reshape it again. If shaped in a pan, the dough should fill half to two-thirds of the pan. Cover with plastic wrap. Leave dough to prove until doubled in size.

Most loaves are cut with decorative slashes before they are placed in the oven so the dough will expand during baking. Do not make the slashes too deep. Glaze the dough with milk, melted butter, or beaten egg for a better finish.

## BAKING

Place pans in the center of an oven preheated to 400–425 °F. Check the bread near the end of baking. When ready, it will sound hollow if you tap the bottom. Use baking times given in recipes as a guide only. If the top of the bread is browning too fast, place a piece of aluminum foil loosely over the loaf.

## COOLING AND STORING

Remove bread immediately from pans and cool on wire racks before slicing.

Bread freezes well for up to three months and can be reheated or thawed in a moderate oven.

Spinach and Cheese Plait (page 48)

## ITALIAN-STYLE CHEESE BREAD

3$\frac{1}{3}$ cups white bread flour
1 tbsp brown sugar
scant $\frac{1}{2}$ tsp salt
2 tsp active dry yeast
$\frac{1}{4}$ cup sun-dried tomatoes, chopped
1 tbsp chopped fresh mixed herbs
or 1 tsp dried
15 black or green olives, pitted
(optional)
$\frac{1}{2}$ cup grated Cheddar cheese
2$\frac{1}{4}$ cups lukewarm water
2 tbsp olive or sunflower oil

**1** Sift flour, sugar, and salt. Add yeast, tomatoes, herbs, olives, and cheese. Add water and oil and stir well to combine.

**2** Spoon mixture into a well-greased 9-inch loaf pan. Cover and leave to prove in a warm place until risen to the top of the pan.

**3** Bake in a preheated oven at 400 °F for 35–40 minutes. Turn out onto a wire rack to cool. Serve with butter if liked.

MAKES 1 LOAF

---

### VARIATION
Substitute olives with 1 small chopped onion.

---

### TIP
To pit olives easily, lay them on a board and roll over them with a heavy rolling pin.

## SEEDED GRANARY BREAD

2 cups whole-wheat bread flour
1$\frac{1}{3}$ cups granary flour
1 tsp salt
2 tsp active dry yeast
2 tbsp sunflower seeds
1 tbsp sesame seeds
about 1$\frac{3}{4}$ cups lukewarm water
1 tbsp honey or corn
syrup
1 tbsp sunflower oil

**1** Mix flours and salt together. Add yeast and seeds.

**2** Add water, honey, and oil and mix into dry ingredients to make a moist dough.

**3** Mix well and spoon into a well-greased 9-inch loaf pan. Cover and let prove in a warm place to double in size.

**4** Bake in a preheated oven at 350 °F for 40–45 minutes. Bake mini loaves for about 30 minutes. Turn out onto a wire rack to cool.

MAKES 1 LOAF

---

### TIP
To test if bread is baked, remove it from the pan, turn it upside down and tap the underside. If it is ready, it should sound hollow, like a drum. If it sounds heavy or dense, return it to the oven to bake for a few more minutes.

## SPINACH AND CHEESE PLAIT

$\frac{1}{4}$ stick butter
1 small onion, chopped
3 cups fresh spinach, chopped
2 tsp chopped fresh thyme
or $\frac{1}{2}$ tsp dried
freshly ground black pepper to taste
2$\frac{3}{4}$ cups self-rising flour
scant $\frac{1}{2}$ tsp salt
scant 2 cups finely grated
Cheddar cheese
$\frac{1}{2}$ cup crumbled feta cheese
scant 1 cup milk

**1** Heat butter in a heavy-based saucepan and sauté onion until soft. Add spinach and cook for a few minutes, stirring, until soft. Add thyme and pepper, remove from heat to cool, then drain off excess water.

**2** Sift flour and salt. Stir in Cheddar cheese and half the feta. Add spinach mixture and enough milk to mix into a soft dough.

**3** Turn dough onto a lightly floured surface and knead lightly until smooth. Divide dough into three long pieces. Plait together on a greased cookie sheet. Sprinkle with remaining feta cheese.

**4** Bake in a preheated oven at 350 °F for 40–45 minutes. This bread can be served warm or cold.

MAKES 1 LARGE BREAD

Left to right: *Seeded Granary Bread (various shapes), Italian-style Cheese Bread.*

## PITA BREADS

*Use pita breads as a base for pizzas.*
*Simply add toppings of choice.*

scant 4 cups white bread flour
1 tsp salt
1 tsp superfine sugar
2 tsp active dry yeast
½ cup warm milk
½ cup plain yogurt
1 large egg, lightly beaten
4 tbsp lukewarm water
1 tbsp sunflower oil

**1** Sift flour and salt. Add sugar and mix. Add yeast.

**2** Whisk remaining ingredients together and mix into dry ingredients. Turn dough onto a lightly floured counter and knead until smooth and elastic. Cover and let prove in a warm place until doubled in size.

**3** Turn dough onto a lightly floured counter and knead until smooth. Divide dough into eight equal portions. Knead each portion into a ball, and press into 8-inch rounds with the palm of your hand.

**4** Place on lightly floured cookie sheets, leaving enough space in between to rise. Let prove in a warm place until risen.

**5** Bake in a preheated oven at 375 °F for about 10 minutes or until bread is lightly browned and the rounds have puffed.

MAKES 8 BREADS

## BASIL AND BELL PEPPER CORNBREAD

1 stick butter
1 onion, chopped
1 red bell pepper, seeded and chopped
1½ cups cornmeal or polenta
1¼ cups all-purpose flour
¼ cup superfine sugar
1 tbsp baking powder
1½ tsp salt
½ tsp baking soda
pinch of cayenne pepper
1¾ cups buttermilk
3 large eggs
½ cup grated mozzarella cheese
14-oz can corn kernels, drained
3 tbsp chopped fresh basil
or 1 tbsp dried

**1** Melt ¼ stick butter in a medium saucepan and sauté onion and red bell pepper until soft. Set aside.

**2** Sift dry ingredients into a large bowl. Add remaining butter and rub in with fingertips until mixture resembles coarse bread crumbs.

**3** Whisk buttermilk and eggs and add to dry mixture. Add cheese, sweetcorn, bell pepper mixture, and basil. Mix well.

**4** Spoon into a greased 10 x 14-inch cookie sheet. Bake in a preheated oven at 400 °F for 20–25 minutes until golden. Let cool in the pan, then cut into fingers or squares.

MAKES ABOUT 28 FINGERS

## SCALLION AND GARLIC ROLLS

5 cups white bread flour
2 tsp salt
2 tsp superfine sugar
2 tsp active dry yeast
4 tbsp chopped scallions
4 cloves garlic, minced
about 1¾ cups lukewarm water
2 tbsp sunflower oil
¼ stick butter or 2 tbsp margarine, melted

**1** Sift flour and salt. Add sugar and mix. Add yeast, scallions, and minced garlic. Add water and oil to dry ingredients to make a soft dough.

**2** Knead on a lightly floured surface until dough is smooth and elastic. Cover and let prove in a warm place until doubled in size. Knead again and divide dough into 12 pieces. Roll each piece into a bun shape.

**3** Brush rolls with melted butter and let prove. Bake in a preheated oven at 350 °F for 20–25 minutes.

MAKES 12 ROLLS

### VARIATION
Substitute fresh garlic with 1 tsp dried garlic flakes.

### TIP
Active dry yeast is easy to use. Sold in most supermarkets, it can be stored for up to 18 months at room temperature.

Clockwise from left: *Scallion and Garlic Rolls, Pita Breads, Basil and Bell Pepper Cornbread.*

51 B R E A D S

## HONEY OAT BREAD

scant 4 cups white or brown
bread flour
1 tsp salt
scant 1 cup rolled oats
2 tsp active dry yeast
1 tbsp sunflower oil
¼ cup honey
about 1¾ cups lukewarm water

**1** Sift flour and salt. Add oats and mix. Add yeast.

**2** Add oil and honey to water and mix into dry ingredients. Spoon into a well-greased 9-inch loaf pan. Cover and let prove in a warm place until doubled in size.

**3** Bake in a preheated oven at 350 °F for 50–60 minutes. Turn out onto a wire rack to cool.

MAKES 1 LOAF

## CARAMEL-PECAN BUNS

scant 4 cups white bread flour
1½ tsp salt
¼ cup superfine sugar
2 tsp active dry yeast
scant 1 cup warm milk
scant 1 cup warm water
3 tbsp sunflower oil

FILLING
½ stick butter or ¼ cup margarine
¼ cup superfine sugar
1 tbsp ground cinnamon
½ cup coarsely chopped pecans
for topping

**1** Sift flour and salt. Add sugar and mix. Add yeast.

**2** Add milk, water, and oil to the dry ingredients and mix to form a soft dough.

**3** Turn onto a lightly floured counter and knead until the dough is smooth and elastic.

**4** Place in a greased or oiled bowl, cover, and let prove in a warm place until doubled in size.

**5** Punch down dough. Turn onto a lightly floured surface and roll out into a rectangular shape of about 14 x 11 inches.

**6** For filling: melt half the butter and brush over surface of dough. Combine sugar and cinnamon and sprinkle over the brushed butter. Roll up like a jelly roll, starting from the long side, then cut into 12–15 slices.

**7** Melt remaining butter and brush it over the slices. Sprinkle nuts over. Place rolls, cut side down, on a greased cookie sheet. Cover and let prove. Bake in a preheated oven at 400 °F for 15–20 minutes, or until light brown.

MAKES 12–15

### TIP
To test whether the dough has risen properly, try gently pressing with your finger. If the dough is ready, it should spring back.

## POT BREAD

9 cups white bread flour
2 tsp salt
2 tsp superfine sugar
2 tsp active dry yeast
½ stick butter or ¼ cup margarine
about 3 cups lukewarm water

**1** Sift flour and salt. Add sugar and mix. Add yeast.

**2** Rub butter into dry ingredients and gradually add water to mix to a soft dough. Add more water if necessary.

**3** Turn out onto a floured counter and knead dough until smooth and elastic. Place dough in an oiled bowl, cover, and let prove until doubled in size.

**4** Punch down the dough and divide it in two. Place each portion in a greased round pan or a heavy-based ovenproof pot, cover, and let prove in a warm place until doubled in size.

**5** Brush the tops with water or milk and bake in preheated oven at 400 °F for 45–50 minutes.

MAKES 2 ROUND BREADS

### VARIATION
Roosterkoek: Follow recipe for pot bread, but divide dough into about 36 pieces and cook on a grill over coals, or in a griddle pan on the stove.

Clockwise from top left: *Pot Bread, Honey Oat Bread, Roosterkoek (Pot Bread variation), Caramel-Pecan Buns.*

## SOFT ROLLS

5 cups white bread flour
1 tsp salt
4 tsp superfine sugar
4 tsp milk powder or coffee creamer
2 tsp active dry yeast
¼ stick butter or 2 tbsp margarine
about 1 cup lukewarm water
beaten egg or milk to glaze
sesame seeds, poppy seeds,
or grated cheese for topping

**1** Sift flour and salt. Add sugar and milk powder and mix. Add yeast.

**2** Rub butter into dry ingredients with your fingertips until mixture resembles fine bread crumbs.

**3** Add just enough water to mix to a soft dough. Turn onto a lightly floured counter and knead for about 10 minutes until the dough is smooth and elastic.

**4** Place dough in an oiled bowl, cover, and let prove until doubled in size.

**5** Punch down dough and divide into 15 equal pieces. Roll each piece into a ball, or shape into long sausages.

**6** Using a rolling pin, roll each ball or sausage of dough into a long oval and roll up tightly, like a jelly roll. Place bread rolls, with seam at bottom, on a greased baking tray.

**7** Cover the tray with oiled plastic wrap and let prove in a warm place until doubled in size.

**8** Brush with beaten egg or milk and sprinkle with sesame seeds, poppy seeds, or grated cheese.

**9** Bake in a preheated oven at 400 °F for 15–20 minutes.

MAKES 15

---

### VARIATION
Plaited bread
1. Follow recipe for soft rolls. After proving the first time, punch down dough and divide into three equal pieces.
2. Roll each piece into a 16-inch long strand.
3. Plait the three strands until all the dough has been used. Seal ends together well. Let prove in a warm place until doubled in size. Brush with beaten egg or milk and sprinkle with poppy seeds.
4. Bake in a preheated oven at 400 °F for 20–25 minutes. Bake mini breads for 15–20 minutes.

---

### TIP
The dough will be sticky when you start kneading, but will become smooth and silky quite quickly. To knead, stretch the dough away from you with the heel of your hand, then turn and repeat the movement. Dough is sufficiently kneaded when the impression of a finger springs back.

---

## SPICY FRUIT BREAD

scant 1 cup mixed dry fruits
4 tbsp rum
5 cups white bread flour
1½ tsp salt
2½ tsp pumpkin pie spice
3 tbsp superfine sugar
2 tsp active dry yeast
about 1¼ cups lukewarm water
2 tbsp melted butter or
sunflower oil

SUGAR GLAZE
⅓ cup water
2 tbsp superfine sugar

**1** Soak cake mix in rum for about 1 hour. Drain.

**2** Sift the flour, salt, and spice. Add sugar and mix. Add yeast. Add the soaked fruits, water and butter and mix to form a dough.

**3** Knead dough until it is smooth and elastic. Shape into a roll to fit into a lightly greased 9-inch loaf pan.

**4** Cover and let prove in a warm place until doubled in size. Bake in a preheated oven at 350 °F for 30–35 minutes until golden brown.

**5** For glaze: heat water and sugar over moderate heat until sugar has dissolved and brush over hot bread.

MAKES 1 LOAF

---

### VARIATION
Substitute rum with strained tea.

Clockwise from top: *Spicy Fruit Bread, Soft Rolls, Plaited Mini Bread.*

## YOGURT BREAD

2¾ cups whole-wheat flour
2 cups cracked wheat
1 tsp salt
1 tsp baking soda
2 tbsp honey
2½ cups natural yogurt
or buttermilk

**1** Sift flour. Add bran left in sifter and add all the other ingredients. Mix well.

**2** Spoon into a greased 9-inch loaf pan. Sprinkle extra cracked wheat over the top.

**3** Bake in a preheated oven at 350 °F for 45–50 minutes. Turn out onto a wire rack to cool.

MAKES 1 LOAF

---

### VARIATION
To make a seed bread: add
3 tbsp poppy seeds.

---

## TOMATO AND ONION COTTAGE BREAD

### FILLING
1 tbsp olive oil
1 medium onion, chopped
1 clove garlic, minced
3 medium tomatoes,
skinned and chopped
1 tbsp chopped fresh oregano
or 1 tsp dried
salt and freshly ground black
pepper to taste

### BREAD
scant 4 cups white bread flour
1½ tsp salt
1 tbsp superfine sugar
2 tsp active dry yeast
1 tbsp olive oil
scant 1 cup warm milk

**1** For filling: heat oil in a heavy-based saucepan. Add onion and garlic and sauté until soft.

**2** Add tomatoes, oregano, and seasoning. Simmer for 10 minutes or until tomatoes have softened and most of the liquid has evaporated. Let cool slightly.

**3** For bread: sift flour and salt into a bowl. Add sugar, yeast, and one-third of tomato filling. Mix. Add oil and enough milk to mix to a soft dough.

**4** Knead dough on a lightly floured counter until smooth and elastic. Place dough in an oiled bowl, cover, and let prove in a warm place until doubled in size.

**5** Turn dough onto a lightly floured counter and knead until smooth. Shape into a round and place on a greased cookie sheet. Cut a large cross in the top of the round and fill with remaining tomato filling. Let prove in a warm place to double in size.

**6** Bake in a preheated oven at 350 °F for 40–45 minutes, or until loaf sounds hollow when tapped on base.

MAKES 1 LARGE ROUND BREAD

---

## MEALIE BREAD

1 stick butter or ½ cup margarine,
melted
scant ½ cup superfine sugar
3 large eggs
2½ cups white bread flour
1 tbsp baking powder
½ tsp salt
1 cup cornmeal or polenta
14-oz can creamed corn kernels
½ cup milk

**1** Cream butter and sugar. Add eggs, one at a time, and beat until light and fluffy.

**2** Sift flour, baking powder, and salt and add to butter mixture. Add cornmeal, corn, and milk and mix well. Spoon mixture into a greased 9-inch loaf pan and bake in a preheated oven at 350 °F for 50–55 minutes. Turn out onto a wire rack to cool.

MAKES 1 LOAF

---

### VARIATIONS
Substitute the creamed corn
with a can of corn kernels,
drained.
Bake in any other containers for
interesting shapes and sizes.

---

Clockwise from top left: *Ciabatta Roll, Tomato and Onion Cottage Bread, Mealie Bread, Yogurt Bread.*

## CIABATTA ROLLS

6¼ cups white bread flour

2 tsp salt

1 tsp superfine sugar

2 tsp active dry yeast

2 tbsp milk

2 tbsp olive oil

about 2 cups warm water

**1** Sift flour and salt. Add sugar and mix. Add yeast. Stir in milk, olive oil, and enough water to make a soft dough.

**2** Knead dough until it becomes smooth and elastic. Cover dough with oiled plastic wrap and let prove in a warm place until doubled in size.

**3** Punch down and divide into six pieces. Shape into ovals and make deep indentations in each roll. Sprinkle with flour, cover, and leave in a warm place until doubled in size.

**4** Bake in a preheated oven at 400 °F for 20–25 minutes.

MAKES 6 LARGE ROLLS

# SWEET TARTS AND PIES

*With the exception of choux pastry, uncooked pastry dough will keep, well wrapped in plastic wrap, in the refrigerator for 2–3 days. Raw pastry dough can be frozen, but it must be allowed to thaw completely before attempting to roll it out, or it may crack. In most cases, pastry can be shaped and frozen before baking, then baked straight from the freezer quite successfully. The secret of successful pastry making lies in accurate measuring, using the correct proportions of fat to flour, and careful handling. Choux pastry is the exception, as all other pastries need to be kept cool. Pastry must rest beforehand, or it will shrink during baking. Most pastries should rest in the refrigerator, well wrapped in plastic wrap. Where a recipe specifies the weight of pastry, this generally refers to the weight of the flour and not the combined weight of all the ingredients. When buying ready-made pastry, however, the weight specified on the package is the combined weight of the ingredients.*

## PASTRY INGREDIENTS

For most pastries, all-purpose flour is used for a light, crisp result. Self-rising flour will produce a soft, spongy pastry. Whole-wheat flour gives heavier dough, which is harder to roll. For whole-wheat pastry use half whole-wheat and half all-purpose flour.

Take care when adding the liquid to dough. Too much will result in a tough end result. Use chilled water and add just enough to bind the dough. Egg yolks are used to enrich pastry.

## MIXING

For most pastries, cold butter has to be rubbed into the flour. The butter is cut into small pieces, then added to the flour. Then, using your fingertips, lightly take small amounts of the mixture and rub into tiny pieces to resemble fine crumbs.

When adding the liquid, sprinkle this evenly over the surface. Don't add all the liquid at once as the amount needed will be determined by the absorbency of the flour. Knead dough lightly for a few seconds.

When using a food processor, first place the flour in the processor, add the butter, and blend for a few seconds. Gradually add water until the dough is just beginning to hold together.

## ROLLING OUT PASTRY

A cool surface, such as marble, is ideal for rolling out pastry. Dust the work counter and rolling pin, never the pastry, very lightly with flour. Roll the dough lightly and evenly in one direction only, until thin. The usual thickness for rolling out pastries is 1/8-inch – puff pastry is sometimes rolled out to 1/4-inch.

## SHAPING PASTRY

Pastry is most often used to line tart pans and to cover pies. Pastry can also be folded around fillings or wrapped around whole boned fish or meat.

## BAKING BLIND

This is when you prebake pastry before adding a filling. Prick the base with a fork, then line with a large piece of waxed paper. Fill with dry beans and bake for 10–15 minutes at a high temperature or until pastry looks set. Remove beans and bake for a further 5 minutes until the pastry is firm and lightly colored.

## GLAZING

Glazing pastry seals the surface and gives a golden brown appearance. Brush lightly with egg yolk beaten with a little water, or use milk.

## GREEK COCONUT TART

½ stick butter or ¼ cup margarine
generous ¼ cup superfine sugar
2 large eggs
½ cup all-purpose flour
scant ½ tsp baking powder
pinch of salt
1¼ cups dry unsweetened coconut
½ cup milk

SYRUP
½ cup granulated sugar
½ cup water
1 tsp vanilla extract

**1** Cream butter and sugar. Add eggs, one at a time, and beat well until light and fluffy. Sift flour, baking powder, and salt and add to butter mixture with the coconut.

**2** Add milk, mix, and pour into a greased 9-inch pie plate. Bake in a preheated oven at 325 °F for 35–40 minutes until golden brown.

**3** For syrup: boil all ingredients together until sugar has dissolved. Pour syrup over hot tart.

MAKES 1 TART

Almond-Pear Pie (page 60)

## CRUSTLESS COCONUT MILK TART

²/₃ cup all-purpose flour
2 cups milk
³/₄ cup superfine sugar
³/₄ cup dry unsweetened coconut
½ stick butter or ¼ cup margarine,
melted
3 large eggs
1 tsp vanilla extract
scant ½ tsp baking powder
pinch of salt

**1** Sift flour and add all remaining ingredients. Mix well. Spoon into a greased 9-inch pie plate. Bake in a preheated oven at 350 °F for 40–45 minutes until light brown. Let cool.

MAKES 1 TART

## ALMOND-PEAR PIE

### PASTRY
²/₃ cup all-purpose flour
scant ½ tsp salt
½ stick butter
½ cup superfine sugar
2 large egg yolks
scant ½ tsp vanilla extract

### FILLING
1 large egg
1 large egg yolk
½ cup superfine sugar
¼ cup all-purpose flour
1 cup milk
½ stick butter or ¼ cup margarine
1 tsp almond extract
¼ cup ground almonds
14-oz can pear halves, drained
¼ cup smooth apricot jelly

**1** For pastry: sift flour and salt together. Rub in butter until the mixture resembles bread crumbs.

**2** Add sugar, egg yolks, and vanilla extract. Mix well, wrap airtight, and refrigerate for about 30 minutes.

**3** Roll out pastry on a lightly floured counter and use to line a greased 9½-inch loose-bottomed tart pan. Prick the base with a fork, line with waxed paper, and fill with dry beans.

**4** Bake blind in a preheated oven at 375 °F for about 10 minutes. Remove from oven. Remove paper and beans.

**5** For filling: beat egg, egg yolk, and sugar until light and fluffy. Sift flour and add to mixture with the milk, beating well. Place in heavy-based saucepan and heat until thickened, about 2–3 minutes.

**6** Remove from heat and add butter, almond extract, and almonds. Set aside to cool slightly.

**7** Fill case with filling and arrange pears on top. Heat jelly and brush over the top of the pie and over the pears. Bake in preheated oven at 350 °F for 15–20 minutes. Cut into wedges to serve.

MAKES 1 PIE

### TIP
Freeze any leftover egg whites, remembering to mark the exact number and date on the freezer bag or sticker.

## APPLE TART

2 large eggs
³/₄ cup superfine sugar
³/₄ stick butter or ⅓ cup margarine,
melted
4 tbsp milk
1 cup self-rising flour
2 large tart apples, peeled and
chopped or sliced

### SAUCE
³/₄ cup evaporated milk
½ cup granulated sugar
2 tsp caramel extract

**1** Beat eggs and sugar until creamy. Add melted butter. Add milk. Sift flour and add.

**2** Add apples and pour the mixture into a greased 9-inch square ovenproof dish.

**3** Bake in a preheated oven at 350 °F for 30–40 minutes.

**4** For sauce: boil milk and sugar over low heat, stirring continuously. Remove from the heat and add caramel extract. Pour the hot sauce over the hot tart. Serve hot or cold.

MAKES 1 TART

### TIP
Sprinkle lemon juice over fresh sliced apple to prevent the apple from discoloring.

**Left to right:** *Crustless Coconut Milk Tart, Apple Tart.*

## APPLE CUSTARD PIE

### PASTRY
1 cup all-purpose flour
¼ cup cornstarch
scant ½ tsp salt
1 stick sweet butter,
cut into small pieces
about 1 tbsp cold water

### FILLING
1 cup heavy cream
3 large egg yolks
½ cup superfine sugar
2 tbsp all-purpose flour
1 tsp vanilla extract

### TOPPING
3 medium tart apples
scant ½ cup smooth apricot jelly

**1** For pastry: sift flour, cornstarch, and salt together. Rub in butter until mixture resembles fine crumbs. Add cold water and mix to a firm dough.

**2** Cover pastry and refrigerate for about 30 minutes.

**3** Roll out pastry on a lightly floured counter and use to line a greased 9½-inch loose-bottomed tart pan. Prick base with a fork, line with waxed paper, and fill with dry beans. Bake blind in a preheated oven at 375 °F for 10 minutes.

**4** Remove from oven. Remove paper and beans. Reduce oven temperature to 350 °F.

**5** For filling: heat the cream in a heavy-based saucepan. Whisk the egg yolk, sugar, and flour together and pour some cream into eggs, whisking all the time. Add egg mixture to saucepan and heat slowly, whisking all the time until it thickens. Remove from heat, add vanilla extract and mix. Cool slightly and spoon into pie shell.

**6** For topping: peel, core, and slice the apples. Arrange on top of custard filling. Heat jelly and brush apple slices.

**7** Bake for 30–35 minutes until the apples are just tender and light golden brown. Cut into wedges to serve.

MAKES 1 PIE

> ### TIP
> Sprinkle apples with cornstarch to prevent discoloration.

## GREEN FIG TART

### SHORTBREAD
1 cup all-purpose flour
¼ cup cornstarch
½ cup superfine sugar
scant ½ tsp salt
1 stick butter
1 tsp vanilla extract

### FILLING
14-oz can evaporated milk
3 large eggs, separated
½ cup superfine sugar
1 tsp vanilla extract
2 tsp gelatin
2 tbsp cold water
⅓ cup red candied cherries,
chopped
5-oz can whole figs in syrup,
drained and roughly chopped
¾ cup chopped pecans

**1** For shortbread: sift dry ingredients. Rub in butter, add vanilla extract, and mix to form a soft dough.

**2** Press pastry into a greased 9-inch pie plate and prick with a fork. Refrigerate for 30 minutes to firm.

**3** Bake in a preheated oven at 325 °F for 30 minutes.

**4** For filling: heat evaporated milk, egg yolks, and sugar in a heavy-based saucepan. Beat constantly until the custard thickens. Remove from heat and add vanilla extract.

**5** Sponge gelatin in cold water. Place in container over hot water and leave until melted. Add to custard mixture.

**6** Whisk egg whites until soft peaks form and add to custard mix. Add cherries, figs, and nuts and mix all together. Spoon into pie shell and refrigerate until set.

MAKES 1 TART

> ### TIP
> Never boil gelatin. Sponge by mixing it into cold water and dissolve over warm water.

Top to bottom: *Green Fig Tart, Apple Custard Pie.*

## QUICK MILK TART

### PASTRY
1 cup all-purpose flour
1 tsp baking powder
pinch of salt
scant ½ cup superfine sugar
¾ stick butter
1 large egg, beaten

### FILLING
generous 3 cups milk
¾ stick butter
¼ cup all-purpose flour
pinch of salt
4 large eggs, separated
scant ½ cup superfine sugar
1 tsp vanilla extract
ground cinnamon for sprinkling

**1** For pastry: sift flour, baking powder and salt. Add sugar. Rub in butter. Add beaten egg, mix well, and press dough into two greased 9-inch pie plates.

**2** For filling: heat milk in a heavy-based saucepan and add butter.

**3** Sift flour and salt, add egg yolks and sugar, and beat well.

**4** Add some boiled milk to the egg mixture, stir, and pour back into saucepan. Boil for a few minutes until thick, stirring constantly, and remove from heat. Add vanilla extract.

**5** Beat egg whites until soft peaks form and fold lightly into the cooked mixture. Pour filling into cases and sprinkle cinnamon over the top. Bake in a preheated oven at 350 °F for 20 minutes.

MAKES 2 TARTS

## CARAMEL-PEPPERMINT TART

### COCONUT PIE SHELL
¾ stick butter
¼ cup superfine sugar
½ cup all-purpose flour
scant ½ tsp salt
6 tbsp dry unsweetened coconut

### FILLING
1 tbsp gelatin
3 tbsp cold water
14-oz can or jar caramel or toffee sauce
1¾ oz peppermint crisp or chocolate mint bar, grated
1 cup heavy cream, whipped

**1** For pie shell: cream butter and sugar together. Sift flour and salt and add to butter mixture with the coconut. Press into a greased 9-inch pie plate. Bake in a preheated oven at 350 °F for 10–12 minutes.

**2** For filling: sponge gelatin in water and dissolve over hot water. Mix remaining filling ingredients and pour into pie shell. Refrigerate until set.

MAKES 1 TART

## MANGO AND PASSION FRUIT PIE

### ALMOND PIE SHELL
¾ stick butter
¼ cup superfine sugar
1 large egg yolk
scant 1 cup all-purpose flour
scant ½ tsp salt
½ cup ground almonds

### FILLING
1 tbsp gelatin
3 tbsp water
14-oz can sliced mangoes in light syrup
1 large egg white
¾ cup passion fruit or mango yogurt
2 tbsp honey
½ cup heavy cream, whipped

**1** For base: cream butter and sugar. Add egg yolk and beat until light and fluffy. Sift flour and add to butter mixture with the salt and almonds. Mix to form a soft dough and press into the bottom and sides of a greased 9½-inch loose-bottomed tart pan.

**2** Bake in preheated oven at 350 °F for 12–15 minutes until golden brown.

**3** For filling: sponge gelatin in water. Place in container over hot water until melted.

**4** Drain the mango syrup into a bowl, add gelatin, and cool. Purée the mangoes and add.

**5** Whisk the egg white until soft peaks form.

**6** Combine the mango mixture, yogurt, and honey and refrigerate. When the mixture begins to set, fold in the whisked egg white and cream and pour into the cooled pie shell.

**7** Set in the refrigerator. Decorate with fruit and extra whipped cream.

MAKES 1 PIE

Clockwise from left: *Creamy Lemon Tart, Ginger and Cherry Pie, Frangipane Tart.*

# FRANGIPANE TART

### RICH PIE DOUGH
1½ cups all-purpose flour
scant ½ tsp salt
1 stick cold butter
1 tbsp superfine sugar
1 large egg yolk
1 tbsp iced water
1 tsp fresh lemon juice

### FILLING
¾ cup smooth apricot jelly
1 stick butter
½ cup superfine sugar
2 large eggs
1½ cups ground almonds
½ tsp almond extract

**1** For pie dough: sift flour and salt. Cut butter into small pieces and rub into flour until the mixture resembles bread crumbs. Add sugar.

**2** Mix egg yolk, water, and lemon juice and add to dry ingredients to make a stiff dough. Knead well.

**3** Wrap dough in plastic wrap and refrigerate for about 30 minutes. Roll out dough on a lightly floured counter to a thickness of ⅛ inch. Press out into a greased 9½-inch loose-bottomed tart pan.

**4** For filling: spread jelly over base. Cream the butter and sugar.

**5** Add eggs, then almonds and almond extract and mix. Spoon mixture over the jelly. Bake in a preheated oven at 350 °F for 20–30 minutes. Cool and serve.

MAKES 1 TART

## TIPS
- After baking, brush the top with warm apricot jelly or brush with a frosting made of confectioner's sugar and hot water mixed to a runny consistency.
- Use leftover pastry to make decorative toppings.

# MUFFINS AND SCONES

## MUFFINS

Muffins are very versatile. Your imagination is the limit to what you can create. Most muffins are quick and easy to make and are absolutely irresistible when served, with or without butter, straight from the oven! They usually taste best on the day they are baked.

### Mixing

A muffin mixture should be handled lightly. The liquid should always be mixed into the dry ingredients, stirring until just combined and moist. The batter should be lumpy. Overmixing will result in coarse muffins, rising with peaks and tunnels.

The muffin recipes in this chapter were all tested using a 12-cup muffin tray (each cup measuring about 3 inches across the top and 1½ inches deep). Other sizes are available and can be used. Just adjust the timing. Grease the cups with a nonstick spray or brush lightly with oil or melted butter.

### Cooling

Muffins are normally baked at a moderate to high temperature. They are ready when they have risen, are browned, and are firm to the touch. Use a metal skewer to check; the skewer should come out clean. Muffins will naturally have cracks on top. Turn muffins onto a wire rack to cool.

### Freezing

To freeze muffins successfully for up to three months, wait for them to cool, then place in airtight freezer bags. To thaw quickly, remove from freezer bag and wrap in foil. Place in a moderate oven for 20 minutes. Alternatively, place each frozen muffin on a paper towel in a microwave on high for 45 seconds. Microwave ovens vary in power, so take care not to overheat.

## BANANA-CINNAMON MUFFINS

2 cups all-purpose flour
1 tsp baking soda
1 tsp baking powder
1 tsp ground cinnamon
scant ½ tsp salt
¾ cup superfine sugar
1 large egg, lightly beaten
¾ stick butter, melted
4 tbsp milk
3 large ripe bananas, mashed

**1** Sift flour, baking soda, baking powder, cinnamon, and salt.

**2** In another bowl, whisk sugar, egg, melted butter, and milk. Add banana and stir this mixture into the flour mixture until moistened; the batter should still be lumpy.

**3** Spoon the mixture into greased muffin cups, filling each one to two-thirds full.

**4** Bake in a preheated oven at 400 °F for about 20 minutes, or until golden brown. Turn out onto a wire rack to cool.

MAKES 12

## CHEESE, BELL PEPPER, AND MUSHROOM MUFFINS

2 cups all-purpose plain flour
1 tbsp baking powder
scant ½ tsp salt
pinch of ground cayenne pepper
1½ cups button mushrooms, chopped
2 tbsp chopped scallions
scant 1 cup grated Cheddar cheese
1 red bell pepper, seeded and chopped
1 tbsp chopped fresh parsley
pinch of freshly ground black pepper
2 large eggs
scant ½ cup sunflower oil
1¼ cups milk
cayenne pepper for topping

**1** Sift flour, baking powder, salt, and cayenne pepper. Add mushrooms, scallions, cheese, red bell pepper, parsley, and black pepper.

**2** In another bowl, whisk eggs, oil, and milk. Add to dry ingredients, mixing until combined. Spoon into greased muffin cups, filling to two-thirds full.

**3** Bake in a preheated oven at 400 °F for 15–20 minutes. Serve warm with butter.

MAKES 12

### VARIATION

Ham and tomato muffins: Omit mushrooms and add ½ cup chopped ham and ¼ cup chopped sun-dried tomatoes.

Cheese, Bell Pepper and Mushroom Muffins

## BEST-EVER BLUEBERRY MUFFINS

2 cups all-purpose flour
2 tsp baking powder
scant ½ tsp salt
¾ cup superfine sugar
½ cup sunflower oil
2 large eggs
½ cup milk
1¾ cups fresh blueberries

**1** Sift flour, baking powder, and salt together. Add sugar.

**2** In another bowl, whisk oil, eggs, and milk and add to flour mixture.

**3** Fold blueberries into mixture; batter should still be lumpy. Spoon mixture into greased muffin cups, filling each to two-thirds full.

**4** Bake in a preheated oven at 400 °F for 20–25 minutes, or until golden brown. Turn out onto a wire rack to cool.

MAKES 10

---

### VARIATION
Substitute blueberries with fresh raspberries.

---

### TIP
Be careful not to overmix the batter as the blueberries can turn the mixture blue.

---

## BACON-CHEDDAR MUFFINS

4 slices rindless bacon, chopped
2 cups all-purpose flour
1 tbsp baking powder
scant ½ tsp salt
pinch of cayenne pepper
1 cup grated Cheddar cheese
1 tbsp chopped fresh parsley
2 large eggs
⅓ cup sunflower oil
1 cup milk

**1** Fry bacon, in a little oil if necessary, and set aside.

**2** Sift flour, baking powder, salt, and cayenne pepper. Add fried bacon, cheese, and parsley.

**3** In another bowl, whisk eggs, oil, and milk together. Add to dry ingredients, mixing until just combined. Spoon into greased muffin cups, filling each to two-thirds full.

**4** Bake in a preheated oven at 400 °F for about 20 minutes, or until golden brown. Cool for a few minutes on a wire rack and serve warm with butter.

MAKES 12

---

### TIP
Freeze the muffins in an airtight freezer bag for up to two months. Place in 750 watt microwave and defrost for about 2 minutes.

---

## APRICOT, ORANGE, AND BUTTERMILK MUFFINS

½ cup dried apricots, chopped
⅓ cup orange juice
2 cups self-rising flour
1 stick butter
½ cup superfine sugar
2 large eggs
scant 1 cup buttermilk

**1** Soak apricots in orange juice for about 30 minutes.

**2** Sift flour and rub in butter until mixture resembles a coarse crumble.

**3** In another bowl, whisk sugar, eggs, and buttermilk and add, with apricot mix, to the flour mixture; the batter should still be lumpy.

**4** Spoon mixture into greased muffin cups, filling each to two-thirds full.

**5** Bake in a preheated oven at 350 °F for 20–25 minutes, or until golden brown. Carefully turn out onto a wire rack to cool.

MAKES 12

---

### TIP
These muffins can be successfully frozen for up to three months.

Left to right: *Apricot, Orange, and Buttermilk Muffins, Best-ever Blueberry Muffins, Bacon-Cheddar Muffins.*

## SPICY CARROT MUFFINS

⅓ cup sunflower oil
½ cup superfine sugar
2 large eggs
½ cup finely grated carrots
¼ cup seedless raisins
scant 1 cup milk
scant ½ tsp vanilla extract
2 cups all-purpose flour
1 tbsp baking powder
1 tsp baking soda
1 tsp pumpkin pie spice
1 tsp ground cinnamon
scant ½ tsp salt
cinnamon-sugar for topping

**1** Beat oil and sugar together. Add eggs and beat until mixture is light and fluffy. Add carrots, raisins, milk and vanilla extract.

**2** Sift the flour, baking powder, baking soda, pumpkin pie spice, cinnamon, and salt together. Add wet mixture to flour mixture and mix until flour is moistened; batter should still be lumpy.

**3** Spoon into greased muffin cups, filling each to two-thirds full. Sprinkle with cinnamon-sugar.

**4** Bake in a preheated oven at 400 °F for about 20 minutes, or until golden brown. Turn out onto a rack to cool.

MAKES 12

> ### VARIATION
> Substitute raisins with chopped nuts, such as walnuts or pecans.

## CITRUS MUFFINS

2 cups all-purpose flour
scant ½ tsp baking soda
1 tbsp baking powder
½ tsp salt
½ cup sunflower oil
scant ½ cup superfine sugar
2 large eggs
½ cup natural yogurt or buttermilk
½ cup grapefruit, orange,
or lemon juice
1 tsp grated grapefruit, orange,
or lemon rind

**1** Sift flour, baking soda, baking powder, and salt together.

**2** In another bowl, whisk oil and sugar together. Add eggs, yogurt, juice, and rind. Fold this mixture into flour mixture; batter should still be lumpy.

**3** Spoon into greased muffin cups, filling each to two-thirds full. Bake in a preheated oven at 400 °F for about 20 minutes. Turn out onto a wire rack to cool.

MAKES 12

> ### VARIATION
> Add 3 tbsp poppy seeds.

> ### TIP
> When grating orange or lemon rind, be careful to remove only the outside rind and not the white pith, which will result in a bitter taste.

## HONEY-GRANOLA MUFFINS

2 cups brown or whole-wheat flour
1 tbsp baking powder
scant ½ tsp salt
½ cup soft brown sugar
¾ cup granola
1 large egg
scant 1 cup milk
⅓ cup sunflower oil
¼ cup honey

**1** Sift flour, baking powder, and salt into a bowl. Add bran left behind in sifter. Add sugar and granola.

**2** In a separate bowl, whisk egg, milk, oil, and honey.

**3** Pour egg mixture into dry ingredients and mix until just combined. Do not overmix; batter should still be lumpy.

**4** Spoon into greased muffin cups, filling each to two-thirds full. Bake in a preheated oven at 400 °F for 15–20 minutes. Cool for a few minutes on a wire rack, then serve warm with butter.

MAKES 10

> ### VARIATION
> For a lighter texture, substitute the brown or whole-meal flour with 1 cup whole-wheat flour and 1 cup all-purpose flour.

Clockwise from left: *Citrus Muffins, Honey-Granola Muffins, Spicy Carrot Muffins.*

## HEALTHY BRAN MUFFINS

2 large eggs
½ cup sunflower oil
2 cups soft brown sugar
2¼ cups milk
1 tsp vanilla extract
1¼ cups whole-wheat flour
1½ cups all-purpose flour
1 tsp salt
2 tsp baking soda
½ cup wheat bran
1 cup mixed dry fruits
1 cup pitted dates, chopped

**1** Whisk eggs, oil, sugar, and milk together. Add vanilla extract.

**2** In a separate bowl, sift flours, salt, and baking soda. Add contents of sifter, then add wheat bran. Add dry fruits and dates.

**3** Add wet mixture to dry ingredients and mix until combined. Spoon into well-greased muffin cups, filling each to two-thirds full. Bake in a preheated oven at 350 °F for 20–25 minutes.

MAKES 24

### VARIATION
Substitute the wheat bran with 1½ cups additional whole-wheat flour.

### TIP
Store the mixture in an airtight container in the refrigerator for up to two weeks.

## CAPPUCCINO MUFFINS

2 cups self-rising flour
scant ½ tsp baking soda
scant ½ tsp salt
1 tbsp instant coffee powder
¾ cup superfine sugar
2 large eggs
½ cup milk
½ cup sunflower oil

**1** Sift flour, baking soda, salt, and coffee powder together. Add sugar.

**2** In another bowl, whisk eggs, milk, and oil together. Fold this mixture into flour mixture; the batter should still be lumpy.

**3** Spoon into greased muffin cups, filling each to two-thirds full. Bake in a preheated oven at 400 °F for about 20 minutes, or until golden brown. Turn out onto a wire rack to cool.

MAKES 10

### VARIATIONS
Add Kahlúa to egg mixture.
To make double chocolate muffins: Omit coffee powder and add ¾ cup chocolate chips, ¼ cup unsweetened cocoa and 4 tbsp milk.

## MANDARIN MUFFINS

1½ cups all-purpose flour
2 tsp baking powder
scant ½ tsp pumpkin pie spice
scant ½ tsp salt
½ cup superfine sugar
1 large egg, beaten
scant 1 cup milk
¾ stick butter, melted
14-oz can mandarin orange segments, drained

**1** Sift together flour, baking powder, pumpkin pie spice and salt. Add sugar.

**2** In another bowl, whisk egg, milk, and melted butter. Add this mixture to dry ingredients, stirring until just combined. Add mandarins and stir in. Do not overmix; the batter should still be lumpy.

**3** Spoon into greased muffin cups, filling each to two-thirds full. Bake in a preheated oven at 400 °F for 15–20 minutes, or until golden brown. Cool for a few minutes on a rack, then serve warm with butter.

MAKES 10

### VARIATION
Substitute mandarins with any other drained, canned fruit of choice.

Left to right: *Healthy Bran Muffins, Mandarin Muffins.*

## SCONES

Scone recipes usually contain an approximate liquid quantity as the moisture content of flour varies and the rate at which the flour absorbs the liquid will determine the amount required. Scone dough must be soft and sticky. When turning onto a lightly floured counter, dust your hands with flour. Don't use too much flour as this will result in dry scones and cause them to brown too much. Flatten the dough gently by hand to achieve an equal overall thickness, or use a rolling pin. Cut with a knife or a metal scone cutter.

The oven temperature should be very hot as scones need to rise quickly.

For a golden brown colour, brush with water, milk, or beaten egg. If crusty scones are required, space them about ½ inch apart. Alternatively, stack them close together on a greased cookie sheet and bake for slightly longer. This will result in upright scones with soft sides. To soften the crust, wrap hot scones in a dish towel.

## CHEDDAR-DILL SCONES

2½ cups all-purpose flour
1 tbsp baking powder
scant ½ tsp salt
1 stick butter or ½ cup margarine
2 tbsp chopped fresh dill
or 2 tsp dried
½ cup grated Cheddar cheese
1 large egg
about ½ cup milk

**1** Sift flour, baking powder, and salt. Rub in butter and add dill and cheese.

**2** In another bowl, beat egg and milk. Mix this into flour mixture until a soft dough is formed. Turn onto a lightly floured counter.

**3** Divide dough in half. Roll each piece into an 8-inch flattened ball. Cut each one into eight wedges.

**4** Bake in a preheated oven at 400 °F for 15–20 minutes until golden brown. Serve hot with butter.

MAKES 16 WEDGES

## ORANGE-PUMPKIN SCONES

3¼ cups all-purpose flour
4 tsp baking powder
scant ½ tsp salt
2 tbsp superfine sugar
4 tbsp milk
4 tbsp fresh orange juice
about 3 tbsp sunflower oil
1 large egg
1 tsp grated orange rind
¾ cup cooked, mashed pumpkin

**1** Sift flour, baking powder, and salt. Add sugar.

**2** In a separate bowl, whisk together milk, orange juice, oil, egg, and rind. Mix this into dry ingredients. Add mashed pumpkin and lightly mix. Roll out to a thickness of ¾ inch. Stamp out with a 7¼-inch scone cutter and bake in a preheated oven at 400 °F for 10–12 minutes. Turn out onto a wire rack to cool.

MAKES 8

> ### VARIATION
> Substitute pumpkin with mashed butternut squash.

## FRUIT SCONES

1 cup hot, strong black tea
½ cup mixed dry fruits
2 cups self-rising flour
scant ½ tsp salt
½ tsp ground cinnamon
pinch of pumpkin pie spice
½ stick butter or ¼ cup margarine
about ½ cup sour cream

**1** Pour tea over fruits and leave for 20 minutes until mixture is cold.

**2** Sift dry ingredients into a bowl and rub in butter. Stir in fruit with ½ cup of the tea and enough sour cream and lightly mix to a soft dough.

**3** Turn dough onto a floured counter. Press out to ¾-inch thick and cut with a 2½-inch scone cutter. Place on a greased cookie sheet. Bake in a preheated oven at 400 °F for 12–15 minutes. Cool.

MAKES 10

> ### TIP
> Pack raw scones tightly together on a cookie sheet for a softer, more moist result.

Clockwise from left: *Fruit Scones, Cheddar-Dill Scones, Orange-Pumpkin Scones.*

## BUTTERMILK SCONES

2 cups all-purpose plain flour
1 tbsp baking powder
scant ½ tsp salt
2 tbsp superfine sugar
1 stick butter
1 large egg
½ cup buttermilk or sour cream
3½ tbsp water

**1** Sift flour, baking powder, and salt together. Add the superfine sugar. Rub in butter until the mixture resembles fine bread crumbs.

**2** In a separate bowl, whisk egg, buttermilk, and water.

**3** Make a well in the center of the flour mixture and pour in liquid. Mix to form a soft dough. Turn onto a lightly floured counter, pat lightly to ¾ inch thick and cut into rounds with a 2½-inch scone cutter.

**4** Place scones on a greased cookie sheet. Bake in a preheated oven at 400 °F for 12–15 minutes. Turn out onto a wire rack to cool.

MAKES ABOUT 10

### VARIATIONS
Cheese scones: Add ¾ cup grated Cheddar cheese to dough.
Herb scones: Add chopped fresh herbs to dry ingredients.
Date or nut scones: Add ½ cup chopped dates or nuts.

### TIP
Buttermilk is an excellent baking ingredient. It can be substituted by adding 1 tbsp fresh lemon juice or vinegar to every 1 cup milk. Let the mixture stand for about 5 minutes to thicken.

# PIES AND MAIN COURSE BAKES

*Puff pastry is most successfully made with strong flour, with a little lemon juice added to soften the gluten and make the dough more elastic. Rolling and folding also form part of the method. Traditionally, shortcrust pastry is made with a mix of butter and lard, but today it is more often made with butter only for a richer flavour. If margarine is used, it should be the hard, block type.*

## PUFF PASTRY

2½ cups white bread flour
scant ½ tsp salt
2 sticks cold butter
½ cup iced water
1 tsp fresh lemon juice

**1** Sift flour and salt. Press butter into a 6-inch flat square and keep chilled.

**2** Mix water with lemon juice, pour over flour, and cut in with a knife. Mix until smooth, forming a stiff dough.

**3** Roll out pastry on a lightly floured counter to a thickness of ¼ inch, keeping it rectangular.

**4** Place butter in center of dough and fold corners to the middle to make an envelope, enclosing butter.

**5** Roll out pastry again. Fold in three by turning bottom third up and top third over the previous fold. Seal edges, then roll and fold in three again. Chill for 30 minutes.

**6** Repeat rolling and folding pastry seven times, chilling when necessary.

**7** Roll out and refrigerate for at least 30 minutes before using, or freeze for up to three months.

MAKES ABOUT 1 LB 5 OZ PASTRY

## CREAMY BACON PLAIT

½ stick butter or ¼ cup margarine
2 tbsp all-purpose flour
1 cup milk
1 tbsp sunflower oil
4 slices rindless bacon, chopped
1 medium onion, chopped
1 medium green bell pepper,
seeded and chopped
1½ cups button mushrooms,
sliced (optional)
2 tsp chopped fresh mixed herbs
or ½ tsp dried
salt and freshly ground black
pepper to taste
10½ oz puff pastry (see left)
beaten egg or milk to glaze
2 tbsp sesame seeds for topping

**1** Melt butter in a saucepan. Add flour, stirring over low heat for 1 minute. Add milk, stirring constantly until smooth and thick. Set aside.

**2** Heat oil in a saucepan and fry bacon until crisp. Add onion, green bell pepper, and mushrooms and sauté until just soft. Add herbs, salt, and pepper and let cool slightly.

**3** Roll out pastry to a thickness of ⅛ inch and shape into a rectangle.

**4** Mix white sauce and bacon mixture. Spoon into center of pastry, leaving both sides open.

**5** Cut sides diagonally into about ⅝-inch strips and plait by folding over filling. Place on a greased cookie sheet. Brush with beaten egg or milk and sprinkle with sesame seeds. Bake in a preheated oven at 400 °F for 30–35 minutes.

SERVES 4–6

## CHIVE-ONION TWISTS

1 tbsp butter
1 medium onion, finely chopped
4 tbsp chopped fresh chives
10½ oz puff pastry (see far left)
1 tbsp milk
½ cup grated Cheddar cheese

**1** Melt butter in a saucepan. Sauté onion and chives until soft. Set aside.

**2** Roll pastry into a ⅛-inch thick rectangle. Spread onion mixture over one half. Cover with remaining pastry. Brush with milk and sprinkle with cheese. Roll lightly.

**3** Cut pastry into ¾-inch wide strips of about 7¼ inches in length. Twist strips and place on greased cookie sheets. Brush lightly with milk. Bake in a preheated oven at 400 °F for 12–15 minutes.

MAKES 14

Creamy Bacon Plait

## VENISON AND BACON PIE

10½ oz puff pastry (see page 80)
1 large egg, beaten

MARINADE
½ cup dry red wine
½ cup buttermilk
1 tbsp Worcestershire sauce
(optional)

FILLING
3 lb 3 oz venison, cubed
3½ tbsp sunflower oil
2 large onions, coarsely chopped
8 slices rindless bacon, chopped
3–4 cloves garlic, minced
about 3 cups meat broth
½ cup red wine
1 tbsp chopped fresh thyme
or 1 tsp dried
salt and freshly ground black
pepper to taste
5 carrots, quartered, or
1¼ cups baby carrots

**1**  For marinade: mix all ingredients well. Marinate venison overnight, or for at least 6 hours.

**2**  For filling: heat oil in a large, heavy-based saucepan and sauté onions, bacon, and garlic until soft. Remove venison from marinade with a slotted spoon. Add to onion mixture and brown.

**3**  Add broth, wine, thyme, and seasoning. Bring to a boil, reduce heat, and simmer for 2½–3 hours. Add more broth if necessary.

**4**  Add carrots and simmer for a further 20 minutes. Thicken slightly with flour if necessary. Spoon into a large ovenproof dish. Roll out pastry to a thickness of ⅛ inch and cover dish. Crimp edges and brush with egg. Bake in a preheated oven at 425 °F for 15–20 minutes, or until pastry is golden brown.

SERVES 4–6

---

### VARIATION
Make mini pies in deep bun pans and bake for about 20 minutes.

---

### TIP
The flavor of garlic, like that of onion, softens if you simmer it in liquid.

---

## FRUITY PORK PIE

2 tbsp sunflower oil
1 lb 2 oz pork sausages
1 large onion, chopped
2 medium potatoes, cut into cubes
½ cup seedless raisins
1 tbsp chopped fresh oregano
or 1 tsp dried
scant ½ tsp ground cinnamon
1 cup beef broth
2 tart apples, peeled,
cored, and sliced
½ cup apple juice
1 tbsp all-purpose flour
salt and freshly ground black
pepper to taste
10½ oz puff pastry (see page 80)
beaten egg or milk to glaze

**1**  Heat oil in a heavy-based saucepan. Brown sausages; remove and cut into slices.

**2**  Return sausages to saucepan. Stir in onion, potatoes, raisins, oregano, and cinnamon and cook for a few minutes over medium heat.

**3**  Add broth, apples, and apple juice. Cover and simmer for 10–15 minutes.

**4**  Mix flour with 2 tbsp water, add to mixture, and boil until it thickens. Add seasoning and let cool.

**5**  Roll half the pastry to a thickness of ⅛ inch and line a large greased pie plate. Fill with cooked mixture.

**6**  Roll out remainder of dough to a thickness of ⅛ inch and cover pie. Seal edges with water and slash pastry lid with a knife or lattice pastry cutter. Brush with beaten egg or milk.

**7**  Bake in a preheated oven at 400 °F for 30–40 minutes.

SERVES 6

---

### VARIATION
Make individual pies.

---

### TIP
If pastry takes too long to brown and the filling boils out, add a little dried milk and superfine sugar to the dough recipe the next time you make it. The pastry will taste nice and will brown quickly.

Left to right: *Fruity Pork Pies, Venison and Bacon Pie.*

## CRUSTLESS ASPARAGUS PIE

¾ stick butter
1 onion, chopped
⅔ cup all-purpose flour
10-oz can asparagus pieces
2¼ cups milk
1 cup crumbled feta cheese
1½ cups button mushrooms, sliced
2 tbsp chopped fresh parsley
or 2 tsp dried
1 tsp prepared mustard
scant ½ tsp salt
pinch of cayenne pepper
3 large eggs, beaten

**1**  Heat 1 tbsp butter in a heavy-based saucepan. Add onion and sauté until soft. Remove and set aside.

**2**  Melt remaining butter and stir in flour. Drain asparagus liquid from can and add with milk to butter mixture. Boil until it thickens.

**3**  Remove from heat and add fried onion, asparagus, and all remaining ingredients. Stir gently to prevent asparagus breaking up.

**4**  Spoon into a 9½-inch square ovenproof dish. Bake in a preheated oven at 350 °F for 30–40 minutes until golden.

SERVES 4–6

---

### TIP
To preserve herbs, hang them in a dry, dark place. This concentrates the essential oils and provides a store of flavor for cooking.

---

## CHICKEN AND PASTA PIE

2½ cups pasta shells
4 chicken breasts, skinned
and boned (about 1 lb 2 oz)
1 tbsp sunflower oil
4 slices rindless bacon, chopped
2 medium onions, chopped
salt and freshly ground black
pepper to taste
¼ stick butter or 1 tbsp margarine
¼ cup all-purpose flour
2½ cups milk

TOPPING
½ cup grated mozzarella cheese
1 tbsp dry bread crumbs

**1**  Cook pasta, drain, and set aside. Simmer chicken in a little broth or water until cooked, then drain and cut into small pieces.

**2**  Heat oil in heavy-based saucepan and sauté bacon and onions until soft. Add chicken, pasta, and seasoning, mix and spoon into a 9½-inch square ovenproof dish.

**3**  Heat butter in a heavy-based saucepan. Add flour and stir over heat for a minute. Add milk and stir while boiling until it thickens. Pour over chicken mixture.

**4**  For topping: sprinkle cheese and crumbs over the top of the pie and bake in a preheated oven at 350 °F for 15–20 minutes.

SERVES 4–6

---

## BACON FRITTERS

1½ cups self-rising flour
½ tsp salt
1 cup milk
2 large eggs
scant 1 cup grated Cheddar cheese
4 slices rindless bacon, chopped
and fried
1 tbsp chopped fresh parsley
or 1 tsp dried
oil for frying

**1**  Sift flour and salt together. In another bowl, whisk milk and eggs and beat gradually into flour mixture.

**2**  Add cheese, bacon, and parsley and mix lightly.

**3**  Shallow-fry tablespoonfuls of mixture in hot oil until brown on both sides. Serve hot.

MAKES ABOUT 15

---

### VARIATION
Substitute cheese and bacon with 6-oz can tuna, drained, or 14-oz can creamed corn kernels.

---

### TIP
Fry the fritters in hot oil. If the oil is too cold, too much of the oil will be soaked up and will result in soggy fritters.

Clockwise from top: *Crustless Asparagus Pie, Chicken and Pasta Pie, Bacon Fritters.*

## CRUMBED CHICKEN STRIPS

1 lb 2 oz skinned and boned
chicken breasts, cut into strips
1 cup all-purpose flour
2 large eggs, beaten
3½ cups dry bread crumbs
½ stick butter or ¼ cup margarine
½ cup olive oil
2 cloves garlic, minced

**1** Coat strips of chicken in flour.
Dip into beaten egg, then into bread
crumbs. Refrigerate for at least 30
minutes for crumbs to set.

**2** Heat butter and olive oil in a
heavy-based skillet. Add minced garlic
and fry chicken in batches until
golden brown.

**3** Remove each batch and drain
on paper towels. Serve with freshly
squeezed lemon juice or any sauce
of choice.

SERVES 4-6

### VARIATIONS
Substitute the chicken with
steak or fish.
The crumbed chicken can also
be deep-fried.

### TIP
To make dry bread crumbs, bake
slices of bread in an oven until
crisp, then crush with a rolling pin.
Store in an airtight container for
up to one month.

## POTATO BAKE

2 large potatoes
1 cup sour cream
½ cup grated Cheddar cheese
14-oz can cream of chicken soup
2 tbsp chopped scallions
salt and freshly ground black
pepper to taste
1 cup dry bread crumbs
¼ cup whole-wheat flour
¼ stick butter or 1 tbsp
margarine, melted
1 tbsp chopped fresh parsley
or 1 tsp dried

**1** Peel and slice the potatoes and
parboil slightly. Layer them in a large
ovenproof dish.

**2** Mix sour cream, cheese, soup,
onions, and seasoning and pour over
the potatoes.

**3** Mix crumbs, flour, and butter and
sprinkle over potatoes. Top with parsley.

**4** Bake in a preheated oven at 350 °F
for 40 minutes.

SERVES 4

### VARIATIONS
Substitute Cheddar cheese with
any other cheese of choice.
Substitute cream of chicken soup
with any other flavor.

## CHEESE AND CHILE PUFFS

1 cup self-rising flour
1 tsp baking powder
pinch of salt
scant ½ tsp mustard powder
1½ tsp crushed dried chiles
¾ cup grated Cheddar cheese
1 large egg
½ cup milk
1 tbsp butter or margarine, melted

**1** Sift flour, baking powder, salt,
and mustard powder together. Add
crushed chiles and cheese.

**2** In another bowl, whisk egg, milk,
and melted butter.

**3** Add to dry ingredients and mix
until just combined.

**4** Spoon into greased deep bun
pans and bake in a preheated oven
at 400 °F for 10–12 minutes. Serve
warm.

MAKES ABOUT 12 SMALL OR 6 LARGE

### VARIATIONS
Substitute dried chiles with scant
½ tsp cayenne pepper.
Add a few pieces of chopped
ham or bacon if liked.

Clockwise from top left: *Cheese and Chile Puffs, Crumbed Chicken Strips, Camembert Fritters.*

## CAMEMBERT FRITTERS

¼ cup all-purpose flour
scant ½ tsp paprika
4½ oz camembert cheese, cut into
8 wedges
2 large eggs, beaten
⅔ cup dry bread crumbs
oil for deep-frying

**1** Sift flour and paprika. Dip cheese wedges into flour mix.

**2** Dip into egg then breadcrumbs. Press well to coat completely.

**3** Refrigerate for 30 minutes to set and prevent crumbs from falling off.

**4** Deep-fry in hot oil for about 2 minutes until golden brown. Drain on paper towels and serve immediately as an appetizer.

SERVES 4

### TIP
If you are making these fritters for a special meal, try and find the traditional Camembert de Normandie. It has a creamy texture and a soft, white bloomy rind when ripe.

## ONION RINGS IN BATTER

2 large onions, cut into thick rings
extra flour for coating
oil for deep-frying

### BATTER
1½ cups self-rising flour
½ tsp salt
1 tsp paprika
1 tbsp poppy seeds or sesame seeds
1 cup water or beer

**1** Sift flour, salt, and paprika. Add seeds and water. Mix well and let stand for at least 30 minutes.

**2** Dip onion rings into extra flour, then into batter, and deep fry in hot oil until golden. Serve with tartare sauce or sweet-and-sour sauce.

SERVES 4–6

## TANDOORI CHICKEN WRAPS

### FILLING
4 chicken breasts, skinned and boned (about 1 lb 5 oz)
3 tbsp fresh lemon juice

### MARINADE
1 onion, chopped
3 cloves garlic, minced
2 tbsp chopped fresh gingerroot
½ tsp turmeric
1 green chile, seeded and chopped
2 tsp curry powder
scant ½ tsp ground cumin
¾ cup natural yogurt

### DOUGH
3¼ cups all-purpose flour
2 tsp baking powder
scant ½ tsp salt
2 tbsp olive or sunflower oil
1 tsp white vinegar
about 1 cup lukewarm water
½ stick butter
extra butter for frying

**1** For filling: cut chicken into large cubes. Sprinkle with lemon juice and set aside for about 10 minutes.

**2** For marinade: mix together all ingredients and pour over chicken pieces. Cover and let marinate for 4–6 hours, or overnight if possible.

**3** For dough: sift flour, baking powder, and salt together.

**4** Mix oil, vinegar, and water and mix into dry ingredients. Knead dough until soft and elastic. Roll out on a floured counter until about ¼ inch thick.

**5** Spread with butter and roll up tightly like a jelly roll. Cut into 2-inch thick slices (about 12 slices). Flatten each slice slightly by hand and roll out into 9-inch rounds. Let rest for 20–30 minutes.

**6** Heat a skillet and fry dough rounds in butter for 1 minute per side. Remove chicken from marinade and fry until cooked. Fill fried pastries and roll up.

MAKES 12–14

---

### VARIATION
Fill with roasted vegetables.

---

## FISH PIE

### POTATO SHELL
1 cup all-purpose flour
1½ tsp baking powder
scant ½ tsp salt
½ stick butter or ¼ cup margarine, melted
3 cups mashed potato

### FILLING
1 tbsp butter
1 onion, chopped
2 tbsp all-purpose flour
1 cup milk
2 large eggs
2 hard-cooked eggs, chopped
2 x 6-oz cans tuna chunks in water, drained
1 tbsp chopped fresh parsley or 1 tsp dried
1 tbsp chopped fresh mixed herbs or 1 tsp dried
salt and freshly ground black pepper to taste
pinch of cayenne pepper

**1** For shell: sift dry ingredients. Add butter and mashed potato. Mix well. Press into base and sides of a greased 9½-inch square ovenproof dish.

**2** For filling: heat butter in a heavy-based skillet and sauté onion until soft. Mix in all other ingredients and spoon into potato case. Bake in a preheated oven at 350 °F for 35–40 minutes.

SERVES 4–6

---

### TIP
To avoid tears when chopping onions, chill them before chopping.

---

Clockwise from top: *Fish Pie, Onion Rings in Batter, Tandoori Chicken Wraps.*

# GROUND BEEF PIE WITH COBBLER TOPPING

### FILLING

1 lb 2 oz lean ground beef
4 slices rindless bacon, chopped
2 onions, chopped
2 sticks celery, chopped
1 green bell pepper, seeded
and chopped
2 tbsp tomato paste
2 tsp superfine sugar
1 cup meat broth
4 tbsp dry red wine (optional)
salt and freshly ground black
pepper to taste

### TOPPING

1½ cups self-rising flour
1 tsp salt
4 tbsp wheat bran
2 tbsp chopped fresh chives
or 2 tsp dried
1 tbsp chopped fresh parsley
or 1 tsp dried
scant ½ cup grated Cheddar cheese
½ cup milk

**1** For filling: fry ground beef until color changes. Add bacon and fry until starting to brown. Add onions, celery, and green bell pepper and sauté until soft.

**2** Add tomato paste, sugar, broth, wine, and seasoning and simmer for about 10 minutes.

**3** For topping: sift the flour and salt and add the bran. Add the chives, parsley, and cheese.

**4** Add milk and mix lightly into a soft dough. Roll out on a lightly floured counter to a thickness of ⅝ inch. Stamp out rounds with a 2½-inch cutter.

**5** Spoon ground beef into a large ovenproof dish and top with scone rounds. Bake in a preheated oven at 350 °F for 30–40 minutes.

SERVES 4–6

---

### TIP

When flouring a counter to knead on or roll out pastry, use a flour shaker to prevent too much flour being absorbed by the pastry.

---

# ZUCCHINI FRITTERS

1 cup grated zucchini
2 large eggs, beaten
1 onion, chopped
¼ cup all-purpose flour
½ cup grated mozzarella cheese
salt and freshly ground black
pepper to taste
oil for frying

**1** Mix together zucchini, eggs, onion, flour, cheese, and seasoning.

**2** Heat the oil in a large saucepan. Drop tablespoonfuls of mixture into the oil and cook for a few minutes on each side, until golden brown. Drain on paper towels and serve hot.

MAKES ABOUT 12

---

# GROUND BEEF VETKOEKIES

2 cups self-rising flour
1 tsp baking powder
1 tsp salt
2 tsp chopped fresh parsley
or ½ tsp dried
2 large eggs
1 cup water
1 tbsp sunflower oil
7 oz lean ground beef
sunflower oil for deep-frying

**1** Sift flour, baking powder, and salt. Add parsley. Beat eggs and water, add to dry ingredients and mix well.

**2** Heat oil in heavy-based saucepan and fry ground beef until the color changes. Add the ground beef to flour mixture and mix well.

**3** Spoon tablespoonfuls into hot oil and deep-fry until light brown.

MAKES ABOUT 30

---

### TIP

Parsley is the best known and most used of all herbs. It enhances the flavor of sauces, soups, stews, and stuffings, and is used as part of a classic bouquet garni.

---

Top to bottom: *Ground Beef Pie with Cobbler Topping, Zucchini Fritters, Ground Beef Vetkoekies.*

## RATATOUILLE CRÊPES

### CRÊPES
1 cup all-purpose flour

scant ½ tsp salt

2 large eggs

⅔ cup water

scant 1 cup milk

### RATATOUILLE FILLING
1 tbsp olive oil

1 onion, sliced

1 clove garlic, minced

1 medium green bell pepper, seeded
and chopped

4 zucchini, chopped

1 tbsp chopped fresh oregano
or 1 tsp dried

2 medium ripe tomatoes, chopped

2 tbsp tomato paste

salt and freshly ground black
pepper to taste

2 tbsp freshly grated
Parmesan cheese

**1** For crêpes: sift flour and salt.
Whisk eggs with water and add to
flour with enough milk to make a thin
batter. Set aside for at least 1 hour.

**2** Lightly oil a heavy-based skillet and
heat. For each crêpe, pour in enough
batter to cover base of skillet and fry
until lightly browned on both sides.

**3** For filling: heat oil, add onion and
garlic, and sauté until soft. Add bell
pepper, zucchini, oregano, tomatoes,
paste, and seasoning. Heat until soft.

**4** Spoon the filling onto the crêpes,
sprinkle with cheese, and fold into
quarters or roll up.

MAKES ABOUT 15

## LEEK PIES

### CREAM CHEESE PASTRY
1 cup all-purpose flour

scant ½ tsp salt

¾ stick butter

scant ½ cup cream cheese

1 tsp poppy or sesame seeds

### FILLING
¼ stick butter

2 medium leeks, thinly sliced

1½ cups button mushrooms, sliced

3 tbsp freshly grated Parmesan
cheese

1 cup milk

3 large eggs, lightly beaten

1 tbsp chopped fresh mixed herbs
or 1 tsp dried

salt and freshly ground black
pepper to taste

**1** For pastry: sift flour and salt. Rub in
butter until mixture resembles bread
crumbs. Mix in cream cheese and seeds.
Turn onto a floured board, knead until
smooth, cover, and refrigerate for
30 minutes. Press into tartlet tins.

**2** Line pie shells with waxed paper,
fill with dry beans, and bake in a
preheated oven at 400 °F for about
7 minutes. Remove beans and paper.

**3** For filling: melt butter, add leeks and
mushrooms, and fry until soft. Spoon
mixture into pie shells and sprinkle with
cheese. Mix milk, eggs, herbs, and
seasoning and pour over cheese. Bake
in a preheated oven at 350 °F for
20–25 minutes.

MAKES 6 SMALL PIES OR 1 LARGE PIE

## BOBOTIE PIE

### SWEET POTATO SHELL
1 cup self-rising flour

½ tsp salt

½ stick butter or ¼ cup margarine

3 cups cooked, mashed
sweet potatoes

1 large egg yolk, beaten

### FILLING
2 tbsp sunflower oil

1 lb 2 oz lean ground beef

1 onion, chopped

2 cloves garlic, minced

½ tsp ground ginger

1 tbsp fruit chutney

2 tsp mild curry powder

1 tbsp chopped fresh mixed herbs
or 1 tsp dried

pinch of turmeric

⅓ cup dried apricots

1¾ cups milk

2 large eggs, lightly beaten

salt and freshly ground black
pepper to taste

**1** For shell: sift flour and salt. Rub
in butter and add sweet potatoes.
Mix with egg yolk and press onto
the greased bottom and sides of
a 9½-inch ovenproof dish. Bake in
a preheated oven at 350 °F for
10 minutes.

**2** For filling: heat oil in a heavy-
based saucepan and fry ground beef
until color changes. Add onion and
garlic and sauté until soft.

**3** Add remaining ingredients, mix
well, and spoon into case. Bake for
35–40 minutes until set.

SERVES 4–6

Clockwise from top: *Leek Pies, Bobotie Pie, Ratatouille Crêpes.*

# VEGETABLE QUICHE

### CHEESE PASTRY
½ cup all-purpose flour
½ cup whole-wheat flour
scant 1 cup grated Cheddar cheese
1 stick butter
1 tsp poppy seeds

### FILLING
3 zucchini, sliced
scant 1 cup broccoli florets
¼ stick butter
1 clove garlic, minced
¼ cup sun-dried tomatoes, chopped
1 onion, chopped
2 tsp superfine sugar
½ cup sieved cottage cheese
scant 1 cup milk or cream
2 large eggs
2 tbsp chopped fresh mixed herbs
or 2 tsp dried
salt and freshly ground black
pepper to taste
Parmesan cheese for topping

**1**  For pastry: mix all ingredients in a food processor until combined. Press the mixture into a greased 9-inch pie dish.

**2**  For filling: blanch zucchini and broccoli for 1–2 minutes. Drain.

**3**  Heat butter in a heavy-based saucepan and sauté garlic, sun-dried tomatoes, and onion until soft. Add sugar. Spoon the vegetables into the pie shell.

**4**  Beat cottage cheese, milk, eggs, herbs, and seasoning together and pour over vegetables.

**5**  Sprinkle with Parmesan cheese and bake in a preheated oven at 325 °F for 30–40 minutes.

SERVES 4–6

> ### VARIATION
> Substitute sun-dried tomatoes with ½ cup cherry tomatoes.

> ### TIP
> A food processor is ideal for making this pastry. You can prepare pastry ahead and store it in the freezer for a few months.

# GROUND BEEF PIZZA

### BASE
2½ cups white bread flour
scant ½ tsp salt
½ tsp superfine sugar
2 tsp active dry yeast
2 tbsp olive oil
about ½ cup lukewarm water

### GROUND BEEF TOPPING
14-oz can tomato passata
2 cloves garlic, minced
1 green bell pepper, seeded and
sliced
1 lb 2 oz lean ground beef
3 tbsp tomato paste
2 tsp superfine sugar
4 tbsp dry white wine
4 tbsp meat broth
1 tbsp chopped fresh mixed herbs
or 1 tsp dried
salt and freshly ground black
pepper to taste
2 tbsp freshly grated Parmesan
cheese

**1**  For base: sift flour and salt. Add sugar and yeast and mix.

**2**  Add oil and water to mix to a soft dough. Knead until dough is smooth and elastic.

**3**  Cover with oiled plastic wrap and leave in a warm place until doubled in size.

**4**  Punch down and divide in two. Flatten and spread out each piece on a greased 10-inch pizza tin.

**5**  For topping: heat tomato passata, add garlic and green bell pepper, and simmer for a few minutes. Spread onto base. Fry ground beef with all other ingredients, except cheese. Spread on top of pizza. Sprinkle with grated cheese and let prove for about 20 minutes.

**6**  Bake in a preheated oven at 400 °F for 20 minutes.

MAKES 2 LARGE PIZZAS

> ### VARIATION
> Add or substitute other topping ingredients of your choice.

> ### TIP
> Pizzas on a yeast dough base, baked or unbaked, can be frozen successfully for up to one month, provided topping ingredients are suitable for freezing. Bake frozen, cooked pizza in a preheated oven at 400 °F for 15 minutes, and frozen, uncooked pizza for about 30 minutes.

Clockwise from top left: *Ground Beef Pizza, Spinach Pie, Vegetable Quiche.*

## SPINACH PIE

### PIE DOUGH
2 cups all-purpose flour
scant ½ tsp salt
1 stick cold butter
½ cup iced water
1 tsp fresh lemon juice or brandy

### FILLING
2-oz package dry onion
soup mix
1 cup sour cream
12 cups fresh spinach
¼ stick butter or 2 tbsp margarine
1½ cups button mushrooms, sliced
1 cup sieved cottage cheese
3 large eggs, beaten
salt and black pepper to taste
scant ½ tsp mustard powder
½ cup grated Cheddar cheese

**1** For pie dough: sift flour and salt together. Cut butter into small pieces and rub into flour until mixture resembles bread crumbs.

**2** Mix water and lemon juice into mixture to make a stiff dough. Cover with plastic wrap and refrigerate for 30 minutes.

**3** Roll out dough on a lightly floured counter to a thickness of ⅛ inch. Use to line the bottom and sides of a 9½-inch ovenproof dish.

**4** For filling: mix soup powder and sour cream.

**5** Wash spinach, blanch until soft, drain well, and chop finely.

**6** Heat butter and sauté mushrooms. Mix together mushrooms, spinach, and sour cream mixture.

**7** Add the remaining ingredients and mix well.

**8** Spoon filling into pie shell. Bake in a preheated oven at 400 °F for 35–40 minutes.

SERVES 4–6

### TIP
To prevent the smell given off by cabbage, spinach, and cauliflower when cooking, add a couple of bay leaves to the water.

# DESSERTS

*Everyone loves dessert, from light fruit, crêpes, and crumbles, to heavier puddings, pies, baked puddings, and cheesecakes. Most of these recipes can be made the day before and refrigerated until serving time. This will allow simple and quick heating and will release you from spending unnecessary time in the kitchen.*

## GOLDEN DUMPLINGS

### SAUCE
1 ½ cups water
1 cup granulated sugar
2 tbsp corn syrup
¼ stick butter or 2 tbsp margarine
½ tsp pumpkin pie spice

### DOUGH
1 cup self-rising flour
scant ½ tsp salt
scant ½ tsp baking soda
¼ stick butter or 2 tbsp margarine
1 tsp superfine sugar
1 large egg
4 tbsp milk

**1** For sauce: combine all ingredients in a saucepan and stir over moderate heat until the sugar has dissolved.

**2** For dough: sift flour, salt, and baking soda. Rub in butter until crumbly. Add sugar and mix.

**3** Whisk egg and milk together and add to dry ingredients. Mix until a soft dough is formed.

**4** Bring sauce to a boil and spoon teaspoonfuls of dough into it. Reduce heat, cover, and simmer for about 12–15 minutes without removing lid. Serve hot.

SERVES 4–6

## FRUITY PUDDING

2 cups self-rising flour
½ tsp salt
2 tsp baking soda
1 ½ cups superfine sugar
2 large eggs
18-oz can fruit cocktail,
including syrup

### SAUCE
1 cup granulated sugar
6-oz can evaporated milk
1 tsp vanilla extract
½ stick butter or ¼ cup margarine

**1** Sift flour, salt, and baking soda. Add sugar, eggs, and fruit cocktail, including syrup. Mix well.

**2** Pour the mixture into a large, greased ovenproof dish and bake in a preheated oven at 325 °F for about 45 minutes.

**3** For sauce: place all ingredients in a saucepan. Heat gently and stir until the sugar has dissolved. Boil for 1 minute.

**4** Remove pudding from the oven when baked and pour the sauce over the hot pudding.

SERVES 4–6

## SPICY APPLE CRUMBLE

### FILLING
14-oz can apple pie filling
2 tbsp fresh lemon juice
1 ½ tsp ground cinnamon
or pumpkin pie spice
¼ cup seedless raisins

### TOPPING
½ cup brown or whole-wheat flour
¾ cup soft brown sugar
¼ cup rolled oats
¾ stick butter or ⅓ cup margarine

**1** For filling: place apples in a 9-inch greased pie dish. Sprinkle with lemon juice and cinnamon. Top with raisins.

**2** For topping: sift flour. Add bran left over in sifter, and sugar and oats. Rub in butter. The crumble should be fairly coarse.

**3** Sprinkle crumble over apples and bake in a preheated oven at 350 °F for about 20 minutes, or until topping turns light brown and crisp.

SERVES 4–6

Crêpes with Creamy Banana and Caramel (page 102)

## APRICOT STEAMED PUDDING

²/₃ cup apricot jelly
1 stick butter or ½ cup margarine
½ cup superfine sugar
2 large eggs, beaten
½ tsp vanilla extract
1½ cups self-rising flour
scant ½ tsp salt
4 tbsp milk

**1** Grease a 9-cup heatproof pudding bowl. Spoon the jelly into the bottom and set aside.

**2** Cream the butter and sugar. Add eggs, one at a time, beating well after each addition, until light and fluffy. Add vanilla extract.

**3** Sift flour and salt and fold in. Add milk and mix well. Spoon mixture into the bowl and level it with a spoon. Cover the pudding with a double layer of foil or waxed paper and secure with string or a lid.

**4** Half-fill a heavy-based saucepan with boiling water. Place the pudding bowl in the saucepan, cover, and simmer for 1½–2 hours, checking the water to make sure the saucepan doesn't boil dry. Uncover the pudding and turn out onto a plate. Serve hot.

SERVES 4–6

### TIP
It is easy to forget to check the water level. Put 2–3 small pebbles in the bottom of the saucepan; when they rattle loudly, the water level has dropped too low.

## PINEAPPLE AND COCONUT PUDDING

### SAUCE
2 tbsp all-purpose flour
scant 1 cup boiling water
1 cup granulated sugar
scant ½ tsp salt
½ stick butter or ¼ cup margarine
1 tsp lemon extract

### SPONGE
1 large egg
½ cup superfine sugar
1½ cups all-purpose flour
2 tsp baking powder
scant ½ tsp salt
½ cup milk
1 stick butter or ½ cup margarine, melted
14-oz can crushed pineapple
¾ cup dry unsweetened coconut

**1** For sauce: mix together flour, water, sugar, salt, and butter and boil for about 3 minutes. Remove from heat and add lemon extract. Pour into a large ovenproof dish.

**2** For sponge: beat egg and sugar together. Sift flour, baking powder, and salt and fold in, alternating with milk and melted butter. Mix until smooth. Add pineapple and coconut and mix.

**3** Pour sponge mixture over sauce and bake in a preheated oven at 350 °F for about 45 minutes. Serve hot with cream or custard.

SERVES 4–6

## GINGER PUDDING

2 sticks butter or 1 cup margarine
1 large egg
1 cup milk
1 cup superfine sugar
2 cups all-purpose flour
2 tsp baking soda
1 tbsp ground ginger
2 tbsp smooth apricot jelly
4 tbsp chopped candied ginger (optional)

### SYRUP
½ cup granulated sugar
²/₃ cup water
1 tsp vanilla extract
½ stick butter

**1** Melt butter, remove from heat, and add egg, milk, and superfine sugar. Whisk well together.

**2** Sift flour, baking soda, and ginger. Add to butter mixture, with apricot jelly and candied ginger. Mix well and pour into a large, deep ovenproof dish.

**3** Bake in a preheated oven at 350 °F for 20 minutes. Reduce temperature to 325 °F and bake for another 20–25 minutes.

**4** For syrup: melt all ingredients together and pour over pudding as soon as it is taken out of the oven.

SERVES 4–6

Clockwise from top: *Apricot Steamed Pudding, Pineapple and Coconut Pudding, Ginger Pudding.*

99

## STICKY DATE PUDDING

½ cup dried dates, chopped
1 cup water
1½ cups all-purpose flour
½ cup superfine sugar
1½ tsp baking powder
1 tsp baking soda
scant ½ tsp salt
4 tbsp sunflower oil or melted butter
4 tbsp milk
1 large egg

### SAUCE
½ cup milk
½ cup light brown sugar
½ stick butter or ¼ cup margarine

**1** Put dates and water into a saucepan and bring to a boil. Remove from heat. Let stand for 5 minutes to cool.

**2** Sift all dry ingredients together. In another bowl, whisk oil, milk, and egg and add, with date mixture, to dry ingredients. Mix well.

**3** Spoon into a large, greased ovenproof dish. Bake in a preheated oven at 350 °F for 40–45 minutes.

**4** For sauce: mix all ingredients together and boil for 5 minutes. Pour sauce over hot pudding and serve.

SERVES 4–6

---

### TIP
This pudding freezes well for up to three months.

---

## LEMON-SEMOLINA PUDDING

scant ¾ cup semolina
½ cup superfine sugar
1 tsp finely grated lemon rind
4 tbsp fresh lemon juice
30 g (1 oz) melted butter
2 large eggs, separated
1½ cups milk

**1** Sift semolina and add sugar and lemon rind. Add lemon juice, melted butter, and egg yolks. Gradually stir milk into sugar mixture and beat until well mixed.

**2** Whisk the egg whites until soft peaks form and fold lightly into the lemon batter.

**3** Pour into a well-greased medium ovenproof dish. Place the dish in a baking dish or pan of cold water and bake in a preheated oven at 325 °F for 45–55 minutes. Cover with foil for the last 10 minutes. Serve hot with cream or ice cream.

SERVES 4–6

## BUTTERMILK PUDDING

2 large eggs
½ cup superfine sugar
1 tbsp butter or margarine, melted
⅓ cup all-purpose flour
½ tsp baking powder
pinch of salt
1½ cups milk
1 cup buttermilk
1 tsp vanilla extract
grated nutmeg for sprinkling

**1** Cream eggs, sugar, and butter. Sift flour, baking powder, and salt and add. Add milk, buttermilk, and extract and mix. Pour into a greased ovenproof dish and sprinkle nutmeg over the top.

**2** Bake in a preheated oven at 350 °F for 45–60 minutes.

SERVES 4

## CHOCOLATE FUDGE PUDDING

1 cup all-purpose flour
3 tbsp unsweetened cocoa
2 tsp baking powder
½ tsp salt
¾ cup superfine sugar
¼ stick butter, melted
1 cup milk
1 large egg
1 tsp vanilla extract

### TOPPING
3 tbsp unsweetened cocoa
¾ cup superfine sugar
1½ cups boiling water

**1** Sift together flour, cocoa, baking powder, and salt. Add sugar.

**2** In another bowl, mix butter, milk, egg, and extract and beat into dry ingredients until smooth. Pour into a greased medium ovenproof dish.

**3** For topping: sift cocoa and mix with sugar. Sprinkle over dough. Pour boiling water over the top. Bake in a preheated oven at 350 °F for about 50 minutes.

SERVES 4–6

Clockwise from left: *Chocolate Fudge Pudding, Sticky Date Pudding, Lemon-Semolina Pudding.*

101
DESSERTS

## PUMPKIN FRITTERS WITH CARAMEL SAUCE

### FRITTERS
½ cup all-purpose flour
1½ cups cooked, mashed pumpkin
2 tsp baking powder
pinch of salt
1 large egg

### CARAMEL SAUCE
½ cup granulated sugar
½ cup water
½ cup milk
1 tsp caramel extract
4 tsp cornstarch

**1** For fritters: sift the flour and add the remaining ingredients. Mix well. Fry spoonfuls of the batter in shallow oil for a few minutes on each side until golden brown.

**2** For sauce: place all ingredients in a heavy-based saucepan. Mix well and boil until sauce thickens. Pour over fritters and serve warm.

MAKES ABOUT 15

## CRÊPES WITH CREAMY BANANA AND CARAMEL

### CRÊPES
1 cup all-purpose flour
scant ½ tsp salt
2 large eggs
⅔ cup water
scant 1 cup milk

### FILLING
6 bananas, halved lengthwise
1' stick butter
1¼ cups soft brown sugar
2 tbsp fresh lemon juice
½ cup cream
chopped nuts for topping (optional)

**1** For crêpes: sift flour and salt. Whisk eggs with water and milk. Add to dry ingredients and beat to make a thin batter. Let stand for 1 hour.

**2** Lightly oil a heavy-based skillet and heat. For each crêpe, pour in just enough batter to cover base and fry until lightly browned on both sides. Keep warm while making filling.

**3** For filling: sauté bananas in butter until just soft. Add sugar, lemon juice, and cream and cook for 1 minute.

**4** Place filling on each crêpe, roll up, and spoon over the sauce. Sprinkle with nuts if liked.

MAKES 12–15, DEPENDING ON SIZE OF PAN

---

### VARIATIONS
These crêpes would also be delicious with chocolate or raspberry sauce.
Stack about 6 crêpes on top of each other, layered with banana filling.

---

### TIP
Stack unfilled crêpes between layers of waxed paper and freeze.

---

## MALVA PUDDING

½ stick butter or ¼ cup margarine
½ cup superfine sugar
1 large egg
1 tbsp apricot jelly
1 tsp vinegar
1 cup all-purpose flour
½ tsp salt
1 tsp baking soda
1 cup milk

### SAUCE
6-oz can evaporated milk
generous ¼ cup granulated sugar
1 tsp vanilla extract

**1** Cream butter and sugar. Add egg, beating until light and fluffy. Mix in jelly and vinegar. Sift dry ingredients and add, with milk, beating until smooth.

**2** Spoon into a greased medium ovenproof dish and bake in a preheated oven at 350 °F for 30–40 minutes.

**3** For sauce: heat evaporated milk and sugar until sugar dissolves. Remove from heat and add extract.

**4** Pour sauce over the top as soon as the pudding is taken out of the oven.

SERVES 4–6

---

### VARIATION
Substitute evaporated milk with heavy cream.

---

**Left to right:** *Pumpkin Fritters with Caramel Sauce, Malva Pudding.*

# PEAR AND GINGER ROLY-POLY

### BASE
2 cups self-rising flour
scant ½ tsp salt
1 stick butter or ½ cup margarine
about ½ cup cold water

### FILLING
14-oz can pears, drained
and chopped
⅓ cup golden raisins
½ tsp ground ginger
¼ cup superfine sugar

### SYRUP
1½ cups boiling water
⅔ cup granulated sugar
¼ stick butter or 2 tbsp margarine

**1** For base: sift the flour and salt into a bowl. Rub in butter. Add most of the water and mix to a soft dough. Add more water if necessary.

**2** On a lightly floured counter, knead the dough lightly, then roll out to a thickness of about ⅜ inch and about 10 x 12 inches in size.

**3** For filling: put all the ingredients in a small bowl and mix together until the pears are evenly coated with the ginger and sugar.

**4** Spoon the pear mixture evenly over the pastry. Turn up the edges of the dough to hold in the filling and brush dough with water. Roll up like a jelly roll.

**5** Place the roll in a greased, large ovenproof dish.

**6** For syrup: mix all the ingredients and pour over roll. Bake in a preheated oven at 350 °F for 35–45 minutes. Serve with custard.

SERVES 4–6

### VARIATION
Substitute pears with apples and ground ginger with ground cinnamon.

### TIP
Ginger may be fresh, ground, or preserved in syrup or sugar. All of these keep for a long time, except fresh gingerroot, which will only keep up to two months, provided it's kept in a cool, dry place.

# INDIVIDUAL BRANDY PUDDINGS

1 tsp baking soda
1 cup boiling water
generous 1½ cups dried dates, chopped
1 stick butter or ½ cup margarine
1 cup superfine sugar
2 large eggs, beaten
1½ cups all-purpose flour
scant ½ tsp baking powder
½ tsp salt
½ cup chopped pecans

### SAUCE
¼ stick butter
¾ cup granulated sugar
1 cup water
1 tsp vanilla extract
½ cup brandy

**1** Mix the baking soda with boiling water and pour it over the chopped dates.

**2** Cream the butter and sugar, then beat in the eggs.

**3** Sift the flour, baking powder, and salt together. Mix the flour and nuts into butter mixture and finally stir in the date mixture.

**4** Spoon into greased deep bun pans and bake in a preheated oven at 350 °F for 15–20 minutes.

**5** For sauce: mix the butter, sugar, and water and boil until it forms a syrup. Remove from heat and stir in the vanilla extract and brandy. Pour the sauce over the hot puddings and leave to absorb. Serve warm with custard or cream.

SERVES 4–6

### VARIATION
This dessert can be baked in any larger-sized dishes for a variation. If using one large dish, bake for 35–40 minutes.

### TIP
These individual brandy puddings can be frozen in airtight containers for up to three months.

Left to right: *Pear and Ginger Roly-poly, Apple and Carrot Pudding.*

## APPLE AND CARROT PUDDING

1½ cups all-purpose flour

scant ½ tsp salt

1 tsp ground cinnamon

scant ½ tsp ground ginger

½ tsp baking soda

1 tsp baking powder

1 cup superfine sugar

1 stick butter or ½ cup margarine

2 large eggs

1 cup milk

¾ cup grated apple

¾ cup grated carrots

scant ½ cup seedless raisins or chopped pecans

½ cup dry unsweetened coconut

### LEMON SAUCE

½ cup granulated sugar

4 tbsp water

4 tbsp fresh lemon juice

1 tsp grated lemon rind

1 tbsp butter

**1** Sift together flour, salt, cinnamon, ginger, baking soda, and baking powder. Add the sugar. Rub in the butter with your fingertips.

**2** In another bowl, beat the eggs and milk together. Add this mixture to flour mixture, along with apple, carrots, raisins, and coconut. Mix well and spoon into a greased, large ovenproof dish.

**3** Bake in a preheated oven at 350 °F for 40 minutes.

**4** For sauce: in a saucepan, boil sugar, water, lemon juice, and lemon rind together until sugar has dissolved. Add butter and pour sauce over pudding while still hot.

SERVES 4–6

### TIP
To keep nuts fresh, store them in the freezer.

# CELEBRATIONS

*Many of these recipes for special occasions can be prepared in advance, which will leave you with more time on the day.*

## DARK FRUITCAKE

2 sticks butter or 1 cup margarine
1 cup brown sugar
5 large eggs
1 tsp vanilla extract
2 tbsp smooth apricot jelly
4 tbsp brandy
2 cups all-purpose flour
1 tsp ground ginger
1 tsp pumpkin pie spice
1 tsp ground cinnamon
4½ cups mixed dry fruits
1¼ cups red candied cherries,
halved
1 cup whole almonds

**1** Cream butter and sugar. Add eggs and beat well until light and fluffy. Add vanilla extract, jelly, and brandy.

**2** Sift flour and spices. Add flour mix, fruit, cherries, and nuts to creamed mixture. Mix well until all fruit is coated.

**3** Spoon into a well-lined, greased 8-inch cake pan. Bake in a preheated oven at 275 °F for 2½–3 hours. Cool completely in pan before turning out.

MAKES 1 CAKE

### TIP
This fruitcake can be baked up to two months before Christmas. Wrap airtight in plastic wrap and foil and store in a cake pan. Spoon 1 tbsp brandy over it weekly.

## MARZIPAN (ALMOND PASTE)

3½ cups confectioner's sugar
1½ cups ground almonds
½ tsp almond extract
1 large egg yolk (see page 2)
1 tbsp fresh lemon juice
2 tbsp sweet sherry
2 tbsp water
smooth apricot jelly

**1** Sift sugar. Add almonds and almond extract and mix thoroughly.

**2** In another bowl, combine egg yolk, lemon juice and sherry and add to almond mixture. Add water if required.

**3** Sprinkle confectioner's sugar on counter and knead mixture to a smooth paste. Add extra sugar if too soft.

**4** To cover cake: warm apricot jelly and brush over cake. Roll out paste on a counter sprinkled with confectioner's sugar and use a rolling pin to place paste gently over cake.

### ROYAL ICING

1 large egg white (see page 2)
3 cups confectioner's sugar
1 tsp fresh lemon juice

**1** Whisk egg white until foamy. Gradually beat in confectioner's sugar.

**2** When mixture reaches soft peak stage, beat in lemon juice. Continue to add sugar, whisking until stiff.

## SHERRY AND ORANGE CAKE

1 stick butter or ½ cup margarine
1 cup superfine sugar
3 large eggs
2 cups all-purpose flour
1 tbsp baking powder
1 tsp grated orange rind
½ cup fresh orange juice
4 tbsp sweet sherry

### FROSTING
½ stick butter or ¼ cup margarine
2 cups confectioner's sugar
1 tsp orange rind
⅓ cup fresh orange juice
1 tbsp sweet sherry

**1** Cream the butter and sugar together until light and fluffy. Add eggs, beating well after each addition. Sift flour and baking powder together.

**2** Mix orange rind and juice with sherry. Add liquid and dry ingredients alternately to the creamed mixture.

**3** Pour into two well-greased 8-inch cake pans. Bake in a preheated oven at 350 °F for 20–25 minutes. Cool.

**4** For frosting: cream butter, add confectioner's sugar and remaining ingredients, and beat until smooth and creamy. Use to sandwich and frost the cake.

MAKES 1 LARGE CAKE

Spiral Cake (page 110)

## PLUM PUDDING

2 sticks butter or 1 cup margarine

³/₄ cup soft brown sugar

1¹/₂ cups all-purpose flour

¹/₂ tsp salt

scant ¹/₂ tsp ground ginger

pinch of grated nutmeg

scant ¹/₂ tsp ground cinnamon

³/₄ cup fresh white bread crumbs

¹/₃ cup chopped candied peel

3¹/₃ cups mixed dry fruits

¹/₂ cup whole almonds, chopped

1 tart apple, peeled, cored and finely grated

1 tsp finely grated lemon rind

2 tbsp fresh lemon juice

4 tbsp brandy or orange juice

2 large eggs, beaten

¹/₃ cup milk

**1** Cream the butter and sugar. Sift the flour, salt, and spices and add with bread crumbs to the butter mixture. Add the peel, dry fruits, almonds, apple, and lemon rind. Stir well.

**2** In another bowl, whisk the lemon juice, brandy, eggs, and milk. Add to butter mixture and mix well. Spoon into a greased 9-cup heatproof pudding bowl. Cover with a double layer of foil or waxed paper and secure with string or a metal lid.

**3** Half-fill a heavy-based saucepan with boiling water, place the bowl in the saucepan, cover, and simmer for 2–2¹/₂ hours. Check regularly to make sure the saucepan doesn't boil dry. Uncover the pudding and turn out onto a serving plate. Serve hot with sauce of choice.

SERVES 8–10

---

### ORANGE LIQUEUR CUSTARD

2 tbsp custard powder

generous ¹/₄ cup superfine sugar

¹/₂ cup fresh orange juice

1 cup water

4 tbsp cream

1 tsp grated orange rind

1 tbsp Cointreau or Grand Marnier liqueur

**1** Combine the custard powder and sugar in a saucepan. Gradually stir in the orange juice and water. Stir constantly over high heat until the mixture boils and thickens.

**2** Stir in cream, orange rind, and liqueur. Serve hot.

### CINNAMON-BRANDY SAUCE

2 tsp ground cinnamon

2 tsp cornstarch

3 tbsp superfine sugar

1¹/₂ cups water

4 tbsp brandy

1 tbsp butter

**1** Combine cinnamon, cornstarch, and sugar in a saucepan. Gradually stir in water until smooth. Stir constantly over high heat until sauce boils and thickens. Reduce heat and simmer, uncovered, for 2 minutes. Stir in brandy and butter.

---

## CHERRY-PISTACHIO BISCOTTI

¹/₂ stick butter or ¹/₄ cup margarine

³/₄ cup superfine sugar

1 tsp vanilla extract

¹/₂ tsp almond extract

2 large eggs

2 cups all-purpose flour

scant ¹/₂ tsp salt

1 tsp baking powder

scant ²/₃ cup red candied cherries

scant 1 cup pistachios

**1** Cream butter and sugar together. Add extracts, then the eggs, beating until light and fluffy. Sift flour, salt, and baking powder, add, and mix well.

**2** Mix in cherries and nuts by hand. Divide dough in half. Form two logs of about 8³/₄ inches long and place on a greased cookie sheet.

**3** Bake in a preheated oven at 325 °F for 35–40 minutes or until logs are light brown. Remove from oven and reduce temperature to 275 °F. Let cool for about 10 minutes, then cut diagonally into ¹/₂-inch slices.

**4** Return to the oven and bake for 5 minutes on each side. Turn out onto a wire rack to cool. Biscotti can be stored for up to two weeks in an airtight container between sheets of waxed paper.

MAKES ABOUT 30

Clockwise from top left: *Cherry-Pistachio Biscotti, Plum Pudding, Dark Fruitcake (page 106).*

# HOT CROSS BUNS

5 cups white bread flour
1 tsp salt
½ tsp pumpkin pie spice
½ tsp ground cinnamon
¼ cup superfine sugar
½ stick butter or ¼ cup margarine
2 tsp active dry yeast
1½ cups lukewarm milk
1 large egg, lightly beaten
scant ½ cup golden raisins
2 tbsp smooth apricot jelly

### PASTE FOR CROSSES
½ cup all-purpose flour
2 tsp superfine sugar
⅓ cup water

**1** Sift flour, salt, and spices. Add sugar and mix. Rub butter into the flour with fingertips. Add yeast.

**2** Add milk, egg, and golden raisins and mix well. Knead on a lightly floured counter until smooth and elastic, cover, and let prove until doubled in size.

**3** Divide dough into 16 pieces and knead each piece into a round shape. Pack buns close together in a greased pan. Set aside in a warm place to prove until doubled in size.

**4** For paste: mix all ingredients to a smooth paste. Spoon into a pastry bag fitted with a small tip, and pipe crosses onto buns.

**5** Bake in a preheated oven at 400 °F for 20 minutes. Brush tops with hot jelly while buns are still hot.

MAKES 16

# SPIRAL CAKE

### PASTRY BASE
½ stick butter
1 large egg yolk
2 tsp iced water
½ tsp fresh lemon juice
1 cup all-purpose flour
¼ cup confectioner's sugar
1 tbsp apricot jelly

### SPONGE
6 large eggs, separated
¾ cup superfine sugar
½ cup self-rising flour
¼ cup unsweetened cocoa
2 tsp instant coffee powder
(optional)

### BUTTERCREAM
⅓ cup heavy cream
3½ oz white chocolate
1 stick butter
1½ cups confectioner's sugar
1 tbsp sherry

about ¾ cup apricot jelly
toasted slivered almonds

**1** For pastry base: mix butter, egg yolk, iced water, and lemon juice.

**2** Sift flour and confectioner's sugar and add to mix. Mix until well combined and turn out onto a lightly floured surface. Knead until smooth. Roll out on baking parchment and cut a circle of pastry about 8 inches in diameter. Prick with a fork and chill for 15 minutes.

**3** Place pastry on a cookie sheet and bake in a preheated oven at 350 °F 10–12 minutes, or until golden. Cool and spread apricot jelly on top.

**4** For sponge: grease a 9½ x 13½-inch pan. Line the base and sides with waxed paper. Beat egg yolks and superfine sugar until light and fluffy. Sift flour, cocoa, and coffee powder and add to mix, beating well.

**5** Whisk egg whites until soft peaks form and fold in with a metal spoon. Spoon mixture into pan.

**6** Bake at 350 °F for 10–12 minutes until light golden brown. Turn out onto a dish towel sprinkled with superfine sugar. Remove waxed paper and use dish towel to roll from short side. Leave until slightly cooled.

**7** For buttercream: heat cream and add chocolate. Mix until smooth and let cool. Beat butter, sift confectioner's sugar and add, mixing until well combined. Add sherry and mix well. Gradually beat in the chocolate mixture until thick and creamy.

**8** To assemble: unroll cake and cut into strips 2½ inches wide. Spread one strip with some jelly, then buttercream. Roll up again and place, spiral side up, in the center of pastry base. Spread jelly and buttercream over remaining strips (reserve half of buttercream for topping), and continue spiral until pastry base is covered.

**9** Cover and refrigerate for 1 hour. Spread remaining buttercream over the top and decorate with slivered almonds and sifted cocoa.

MAKES 1 LARGE CAKE

Left to right: *Hot Cross Buns, Tiramisu Gâteau (page 114).*

## PINEAPPLE FRUITCAKE

14-oz can crushed pineapple
3⅓ cups mixed dry fruits
⅓ cup dried apricots, chopped
⅔ cup candied cherries
⅓ cup candied pineapple (optional)
¾ cup dried dates, chopped
1 stick butter or ½ cup margarine
¾ cup brown sugar
½ cup sherry
2 large eggs
3¼ cups all-purpose flour
1 tbsp baking powder
scant ½ tsp salt
2 tsp pumpkin pie spice

**1** Mix all the fruit ingredients in a large, heavy-based saucepan. Add butter and sugar and heat slowly for about 10 minutes, until sugar has dissolved. Remove from heat and add sherry. Let cool slightly.

**2** Beat eggs and add to fruit mixture. Sift remaining ingredients and add to fruit mixture. Pour into a lined and greased 9-inch loaf pan.

**3** Bake in a preheated oven at 300 °F for 1 hour. Reduce the temperature to 275 °F and bake for 30–40 minutes more. If top starts browning too much, cover with brown paper or foil.

MAKES 1 CAKE

### VARIATION
Substitute sherry with port, muscat wine, or fruit juice.

## BATTENBURG CAKE

1½ sticks butter
¾ cup superfine sugar
3 large eggs, lightly beaten
2 cups self-rising flour
pinch of salt
scant ½ tsp vanilla extract
scant ½ tsp strawberry extract
a few drops of red food coloring

### TOPPING
3 tbsp smooth apricot jelly
8½ oz marzipan (see page 106)
candied cherries (optional)

**1** Grease and line an 8-inch square cake pan. Divide the pan by placing a piece of folded waxed paper down the center.

**2** Cream butter and sugar. Add eggs and beat until light and fluffy. Sift flour and salt and add. Divide mixture into two bowls. Add vanilla extract to one bowl and strawberry extract and coloring to the other. Spoon each mixture into its own half of the pan. Bake in a preheated oven at 350 °F for 25–30 minutes. Turn onto a rack to cool.

**3** Trim the cakes and cut each half into two even-size lengths. Heat jelly to soften and sandwich halves together with jelly, alternating the colors.

**4** Brush jelly along outside edges. Roll the almond paste into a rectangle large enough to cover the cake. Wrap paste round the cake and seal the edges. Press edges into a decorative pattern and decorate with cherries.

MAKES 1 CAKE

## MINCE PIES

SODA-WATER PASTRY
2 cups all-purpose flour
½ tsp salt
1½ sticks cold butter
⅓ cup iced soda water
1 tbsp fresh lemon juice or brandy

### FILLING
14-oz jar mincemeat
1 large egg white
superfine sugar for sprinkling

**1** For pastry: sift flour and salt together. Rub in butter with fingertips until mixture resembles bread crumbs. Add soda water and lemon juice and mix to a stiff dough.

**2** Wrap in plastic wrap and refrigerate for at least 30 minutes. Roll out dough on a floured surface to a thickness of ⅛ inch. Cut out rounds to line greased tartlet or bun pans.

**3** For filling: place heaping teaspoons of mincemeat into each pastry case. Dampen pastry edges with water, cover with another round of pastry, and seal.

**4** Prick holes in the center of the lid with a fork or sharp knife and brush with lightly beaten egg white or iced water. Bake in a preheated oven at 400 °F for about 15 minutes. Sprinkle with superfine sugar while still warm.

MAKES ABOUT 24

### VARIATION
Substitute pastry lid with crumble or pastry lattice.

Left to right: *Mince Pies, Battenburg Cake, Stollen.*

## STOLLEN

2½ cups white bread flour

½ tsp salt

2 tbsp superfine sugar

2 tsp active dry yeast

½ stick butter

1 large egg, beaten

⅓ cup warm milk

¼ cup pecans, chopped

scant ½ tsp grated lemon rind

¾ cup mixed dry fruits

scant ⅓ cup candied cherries

5½ oz marzipan (see page 106)
(optional)

confectioner's sugar for dusting

**1** Sift flour and salt. Add sugar and yeast. Rub in ¼ stick of butter until mixture resembles fine bread crumbs. Add egg and milk and mix to a soft dough. If necessary add more milk.

**2** Turn onto a floured counter and knead for 10 minutes until dough is smooth and elastic. Place dough in an oiled bowl, cover, and let prove until doubled in size.

**3** Punch down dough, add nuts, rind, fruit, and cherries and knead into dough. Roll out on a lightly floured counter into an oval shape of about 6 x 8 inches.

**4** Knead marzipan until soft. Form a roll to place lengthwise in center of dough. Fold dough over marzipan. Seal edges. Place on a greased cookie sheet with sealed edge on the bottom. Cover with oiled plastic wrap and let prove in a warm place until doubled in size.

**5** Melt butter and brush top of bread. Bake in preheated oven at 350 °F for 35–40 minutes. Cool and dust with confectioner's sugar. Brush with more melted butter and add more confectioner's sugar if liked. Can be stored for 1–2 weeks.

MAKES 1 STOLLEN

## SACHERTORTE

*A rich chocolate sponge encased in rich chocolate frosting.*

1½ sticks butter or margarine
¾ cup superfine sugar
6 large eggs, separated
7 oz semisweet chocolate, melted
1 tbsp rum or sherry
1 tsp vanilla extract
1 cup all-purpose flour
5 tbsp smooth apricot jelly

FROSTING
3½ tbsp water
3½ oz semisweet chocolate
½ stick butter
1 cup confectioner's sugar

**1** Beat butter and sugar until light and fluffy. Add egg yolks, melted chocolate, rum, and vanilla extract.

**2** Whisk egg whites until soft peaks form. Fold with sifted flour into creamed mixture.

**3** Spoon mixture into a lined and greased 9-inch round springform pan. Bake in a preheated oven at 350 °F for 25–35 minutes. Turn out onto a wire rack to cool.

**4** Cut horizontally into two or three layers. Spread layers with apricot jelly and stack on top of each other.

**5** For frosting: heat water, chocolate, and butter in a heavy-based saucepan over medium heat until melted. Stirring constantly, remove from heat and stir in confectioner's sugar. Pour over cake, spread and let set.

MAKES 1 MEDIUM CAKE

---

### VARIATION
Bake in a square pan and cut into small squares to make petit fours.

### TIP
Dip knife in hot water to spread frosting evenly.

---

## TIRAMISU GÂTEAU

round vanilla sponge cake
(see butter cake, page 40)
½ cup strong black coffee
⅓ cup Kahlúa or sherry
2¼ cups sieved cottage cheese
or mascarpone cheese
scant ½ cup superfine sugar
1 cup heavy cream
½ cup chocolate chips
3½ oz semisweet chocolate
confectioner's sugar for dusting

**1** Cut the sponge layer horizontally in half. Use one half to fit the base of an 8 or 9-inch round, loose-bottomed cake pan.

**2** Mix the coffee with Kahlúa, and sprinkle half the mixture over the sponge.

**3** Beat the cottage cheese and sugar together. Whip the cream and fold it into the cheese mixture. Add the chocolate chips.

**4** Spoon half of cheese mixture over the cake base.

**5** Repeat with second sponge layer, coffee, and cream mixture. Chill overnight in the refrigerator.

---

**6** To serve: remove from pan and place on a serving plate. Whip more cream if liked; spread on sides and pipe on top. Make chocolate curls and top cake. Dust with confectioner's sugar and cut into slices.

MAKES 1 LARGE CAKE

### TIPS
- Chocolate curls: put chocolate in the microwave on medium for a few seconds; be careful not to melt it. Make curls using a potato peeler.
- If preferred, make the sponge in advance and freeze.
- Off-cuts or broken pieces can also be used. Make sure entire tin is covered with the sponge.

## CHRISTMAS ALMOND COOKIES

2 sticks butter
¾ cup superfine sugar
1 tsp vanilla extract
2 cups all-purpose flour
1½ cups slivered almonds
confectioner's sugar for rolling

**1** Cream butter and sugar. Add vanilla extract and sifted flour. Add almonds and roll into small balls. Place on a greased cookie sheet and press them lightly with a fork.

**2** Bake in a preheated oven at 400 °F for 10–12 minutes. Roll warm cookies in confectioner's sugar and cool on a wire rack.

MAKES ABOUT 30

Left to right: *Sachertorte, Christmas Shape Cookies, Christmas Almond Cookies.*

## CHRISTMAS SHAPE COOKIES

1 stick butter or ½ cup margarine
¼ cup superfine sugar
½ tsp vanilla extract
1½ cups all-purpose flour
scant ½ tsp salt
1 tbsp milk

### GLACÉ ICING
scant 1 cup confectioner's sugar
about 2 tbsp boiling water
scant ½ tsp vanilla extract
a few drops of food coloring

**1** Cream butter and sugar together. Add vanilla extract.

**2** Sift flour and salt, add to creamed mixture, and knead to form a stiff dough. Add milk if needed. Roll out to a thickness of ¼ inch and, using a Christmas cookie cutter, cut out shapes. If hanging the cookies from a tree, make a hole in the dough.

**3** Place on a greased cookie sheet and bake in a preheated oven at 350 °F for 10–15 minutes, or until light brown on the edges.

**4** Remove cookies from sheet using a palette knife. Place on a rack to cool.

**5** For icing: sift the confectioner's sugar and add enough water to make a smooth consistency. Add the vanilla extract and coloring of choice.

**6** Ice cooled cookies and decorate with hundreds and thousands, silver balls, and chocolate vermicelli. The cookies may also be dipped into melted chocolate before decorating.

MAKES ABOUT 30

# KIDS

*Spending time making cookies, desserts, or any other creative activities should be a magical experience for children. It is important that they learn to use their own initiative and imagination to change things. The section on party cakes should involve the children – do not always leave the cake as a surprise. Basic techniques, such as sifting the ingredients, should be taught so that they have a perception of baking and grow up being able to do something for themselves in the kitchen.*

## ROCKY ROAD COOKIES

1 stick butter
generous ½ cup light brown sugar
2 large eggs
1½ cups all-purpose flour
2 tbsp unsweetened cocoa
scant ½ tsp salt

TOPPING
½ cup marshmallows, chopped
2¾ oz milk chocolate, chopped,
or ½ cup chocolate chips

**1** Cream butter and sugar. Add eggs and beat until light and fluffy.

**2** Sift flour, cocoa, and salt and add to mixture, stirring until well combined. Drop spoonfuls of mixture onto a greased cookie sheet. Bake in a preheated oven at 350 °F for about 8 minutes. Remove from oven.

**3** For topping: sprinkle with marshmallows and chocolate chunks, pressing slightly into cookies. Return to oven for a further 2–3 minutes to melt slightly. Cool on wire racks.

MAKES ABOUT 28

### TIP
When cutting marshmallows, use scissors regularly dipped in flour to prevent sticking.

## PEANUT BUTTER COOKIES

½ stick butter or ¼ cup margarine
6 tbsp smooth or crunchy
peanut butter
¾ cup brown sugar
½ cup superfine sugar
1 large egg
1 cup all-purpose flour
scant ½ tsp salt
1 tsp baking soda

**1** Cream the butter and peanut butter until soft. Add sugars gradually, beating well.

**2** Add egg and beat until light and fluffy. Sift together flour, salt, and baking soda and add to mixture. Mix well.

**3** Shape teaspoonfuls of the mixture into balls and place on lightly greased cookie sheets. Bake in a preheated oven at 350 °F for 8–10 minutes. Turn out onto a wire rack to cool. Store in an airtight container.

MAKES ABOUT 30

### VARIATION
Serve these cookies crumbled over vanilla ice cream for a delicious variation.

## CRUMPETS

2 large eggs
generous ¼ cup superfine sugar
1 cup all-purpose flour
1½ tsp baking powder
scant ½ tsp salt
½ cup milk
¼ stick butter or 2 tbsp margarine,
melted
sunflower oil for frying

**1** Beat eggs and sugar together until light and fluffy.

**2** Sift flour, baking powder, and salt and add to egg mixture. Add milk and melted butter and mix well.

**3** Place spoonfuls of batter in a heated skillet and shallow-fry until light brown on both sides. Serve with butter and grated Cheddar cheese.

MAKES 15–20

### VARIATION
Add four mashed bananas for banana crumpets.

### TIP
Crumpets are best eaten on the day they were made, but they can be frozen for up to two months.

Rocky Road Cookies

## BASIC SPONGE FOR NOVELTY CAKES

*A variety of novelty cake pans is available in specialist kitchen shops. Alternatively, bake a basic sponge and then cut it into the desired shape.*

### HOT MILK SPONGE CAKE
4 large eggs
1¾ cups superfine sugar
2 cups all-purpose flour
1 tbsp baking powder
1 cup milk
¾ stick butter or ½ cup margarine
1 tsp vanilla essence

### BASIC FROSTING
¾ stick soft butter
1¾ cups confectioner's sugar
1 tsp vanilla extract
about 2 tbsp milk
food coloring of choice

### CHOCOLATE FROSTING
¾ stick soft butter
1¾ cups confectioner's sugar
2 tbsp unsweetened cocoa
2 tbsp hot water
scant ½ tsp vanilla extract
about 2 tbsp milk

**1** For sponge: Cream eggs and sugar together until thick and light.

**2** Sift the flour and baking powder together and fold into the egg and sugar mixture.

**3** In a saucepan, heat the milk and butter. Do not boil. Stir milk mixture and vanilla extract into batter. Spoon into two greased 8-inch round cake pans. Bake in a preheated oven at 350 °F, for 25–30 minutes.

**4** For both frostings: beat all the ingredients until smooth and creamy.

**5** Decorate with candy, taking color and size into consideration. You can use silver balls, hundreds and thousands, chocolate chips, vermicelli, liquorice, or fruited gum candy.

MAKES 2 SPONGES

> ### VARIATION
> Chocolate cake: Add 3½ tbsp unsweetened cocoa to dry ingredients. For other flavors, add 1 tsp extract to basic sponge and a few drops of food coloring.

> ### TIP
> The basic sponge can be doubled for baking in a large cake pan.

## PEANUT AND RAISIN SQUARES

1½ sticks butter or ¾ cup margarine
½ cup superfine sugar
⅓ cup seedless raisins
½ cup peanuts
½ cup dry unsweetened coconut
1 cup all-purpose flour

**1** Melt butter in a heavy-based saucepan. Add remaining ingredients and mix well. Press into a greased 6½ x 10½-inch tray bake pan.

**2** Bake in a preheated oven at 350 °F for 20 minutes. Cool completely, then cut into squares.

MAKES ABOUT 18

## VANILLA CUPCAKES

1 stick butter or ½ cup margarine
¾ cup superfine sugar
3 large eggs
1 tsp vanilla extract
2 cups all-purpose flour
1 tbsp baking powder
scant ½ tsp salt
½ cup milk

**1** Beat butter and sugar together. Add eggs and beat until light and creamy. Add vanilla extract.

**2** Sift flour, baking powder, and salt and add, with milk, to egg mixture. Mix well. Fill paper liners in bun pans to two-thirds full.

**3** Bake in a preheated oven at 350 °F for 12–15 minutes.

MAKES ABOUT 24

> ### VARIATIONS
> Substitute vanilla extract with any other flavor, such as lemon or strawberry, and add a few drops of food coloring.
> To make fairy cakes: cut a thin slice from the top of each cup cake and cut it in half. Whip cream with a little superfine sugar until stiff. Spoon cream on top of cut surface and place cut tops on cream to resemble wings. Dust with confectioner's sugar.

*Novelty Cakes*

# COCONUT ICE SLICES

### PASTRY
½ stick butter or ¼ cup margarine
2 tbsp superfine sugar
½ tsp vanilla extract
1 large egg yolk
½ cup all-purpose flour
2 tbsp cornstarch

### FILLING
2 cups dry unsweetened coconut
1 cup superfine sugar
2 large eggs
⅓ cup candied cherries, chopped

### FROSTING
1 cup confectioner's sugar
1 tbsp milk
1 tbsp butter, melted

**1** For pastry: beat butter, sugar, and vanilla extract until creamy. Add egg yolk and beat well. Fold in sifted flour and cornstarch and press into a greased 6½ x 10½-inch tray bake pan.

**2** For filling: combine coconut, sugar, and eggs in a bowl. Add cherries and mix well. Spoon filling evenly over pastry.

**3** Bake in a preheated oven at 350 °F for 25–30 minutes. Cool in pan.

**4** For frosting: sift confectioner's sugar and add milk and melted butter. Mix until smooth and spread over the cooled cake. Cut into slices.

MAKES ABOUT 28

# FRUITY CHOCOLATE COOKIES

2 sticks butter or 1 cup margarine
1 cup superfine sugar
2 large eggs
1 tsp vanilla extract
2 cups self-rising flour
½ tsp salt
2 cups mixed dry fruits
4½ oz semisweet chocolate, coarsely chopped
6 cups cornflakes

**1** Cream butter and sugar. Add eggs and vanilla extract and beat until light and fluffy.

**2** Sift flour and salt and add to egg mixture. Add dry fruits, chocolate, and half the cornflakes.

**3** Crush rest of cornflakes and roll teaspoonfuls of mixture in cornflakes. Place on a greased cookie sheet.

**4** Bake in a preheated oven at 350 °F for 15 minutes, or until light brown.

MAKES ABOUT 70

### VARIATION
Substitute chocolate pieces with chocolate chips.

### TIP
These cookies are very crumbly. Make sure you work very carefully to prevent breakage.

# BANANA-OAT SQUARES

1 stick butter
½ cup light brown sugar
½ cup corn syrup
2 cups rolled oats
½ cup all-purpose flour
½ tsp ground cinnamon
scant ½ tsp ground ginger
½ tsp baking powder
pinch of salt
3 bananas, mashed

**1** Melt butter, sugar, and syrup over low heat. Stir in oats. Sift flour, spices, baking powder, and salt and add to mixture. Stir well.

**2** Add bananas and mix. Turn into a greased 6½ x 10½-inch tray bake pan. Bake in a preheated oven at 350 °F for 20–25 minutes. Cut into squares.

MAKES ABOUT 24

# PLAY DOUGH

2 cups all-purpose flour
2¼ cups water
¾ cup salt
1 tbsp cream of tartar
1 tbsp sunflower oil
¾–1 tsp food coloring of choice

**1** Mix all ingredients, except coloring, in a heavy-based saucepan. Stir over medium heat until it forms a ball.

**2** Cool and knead well. Add coloring and knead again. Store in an airtight container to prevent drying out.

MAKES 1¾ LB

Clockwise from left: *Fruity Chocolate Cookies, Banana-Oat Squares, Coconut Ice Slices.*

## CHEESE AND HERB PUFFS

1 cup self-rising flour
1 tsp baking powder
pinch of salt
scant $\frac{1}{2}$ tsp mustard powder
2 tsp chopped fresh parsley
or $\frac{1}{2}$ tsp dried
$\frac{3}{4}$ cup grated Cheddar cheese
1 large egg
$\frac{1}{2}$ cup milk
1 tbsp butter, melted

**1** Sift together flour, baking powder, salt, and mustard powder. Add parsley and cheese.

**2** In another bowl, whisk egg, milk, and melted butter.

**3** Add wet mixture to dry ingredients and mix until just combined.

**4** Spoon into greased bun pans and bake in a preheated oven at 400 °F for 10–12 minutes. Serve warm.

MAKES ABOUT 12 LARGE OR 24 MINI

---

### VARIATION
Substitute parsley with any other herbs of choice.

---

## GINGERBREAD MEN

1 stick butter
generous $\frac{1}{4}$ cup superfine sugar
6 tbsp corn syrup
$2\frac{3}{4}$ cup all-purpose flour
1 tsp ground ginger
$\frac{1}{2}$ tsp ground cinnamon
2 tsp baking soda
1 large egg

FROSTING
$1\frac{3}{4}$ cups confectioner's sugar
1 tbsp orange juice

**1** Place butter, sugar, and syrup in a heavy-based saucepan. Bring to a boil over moderate heat until sugar has dissolved. Let cool.

**2** Sift flour, spices, and baking soda and add to syrup mix. Add egg and beat well. Mix further, using your hands, to form a stiff dough.

**3** Roll out dough until about $\frac{1}{4}$ inch in thickness. Cut out gingerbread men and place on greased cookie sheets. Bake in preheated oven at 350 °F for about 10 minutes until light brown.

**4** Place on a wire rack to cool.

**5** For frosting: sift confectioner's sugar and add enough orange juice to make a stiff frosting. Put into a pastry bag and frost.

MAKES ABOUT 15

---

### VARIATION
Decorate with currants, chocolate chips, or cherries before baking.

---

## COCONUT JELLY SQUARES

2 cups all-purpose flour
2 tsp baking powder
pinch of salt
$\frac{1}{2}$ cup superfine sugar
$\frac{3}{4}$ stick butter or $\frac{1}{3}$ cup margarine
1 large egg
4 tbsp milk
$\frac{2}{3}$ cup smooth apricot jelly

TOPPING
1 large egg
$\frac{1}{2}$ cup superfine sugar
$1\frac{1}{2}$ cups dry unsweetened coconut
2 tbsp milk
1 tsp vanilla extract

**1** Sift flour, baking powder, salt, and sugar. Rub in butter.

**2** Beat egg and add milk. Mix into dry ingredients. Press into a greased 9 x 13-inch jelly roll tin. Spread with jelly.

**3** For topping: beat egg, add sugar and beat again. Add the remaining ingredients. Spread on top of jelly. Bake in a preheated oven at 400 °F for 15–20 minutes. Cut into squares while still warm.

MAKES ABOUT 30

Left to right: *Cheese and Herb Puffs, Coconut Jelly Squares, Gumdrop Cookies.*

## GUMDROP COOKIES

2 sticks butter, softened

¾ cup superfine sugar

1 tsp vanilla extract

1 large egg

1½ cups all-purpose flour

½ tsp baking powder

½ tsp baking soda

scant ½ tsp salt

1½ cups rolled oats

1 cup gumdrops, chopped

**1** Cream the butter, sugar, and vanilla extract. Add the egg and beat until light and fluffy.

**2** Sift the flour, baking powder, baking soda, and salt. Add to the egg mixture. Add the oats and gumdrops and mix well.

**3** Drop heaping teaspoonfuls onto a greased cookie sheet, leaving enough space for spreading.

**4** Bake in a preheated oven at 350 °F for 10–12 minutes. Cool on wire racks.

MAKES ABOUT 30

| TIP |
| --- |
| To cut gumdrops easily, use kitchen scissors dipped in cold water. |

# GENERAL MISTAKES AND CAUSES

## CAKES

**Cake has risen unevenly in oven.**
- Flour not blended sufficiently into main mixture.
- Oven temperature too high.
- Sides of pan unevenly greased.

**Cake sinks in center.**
- Too much sugar.
- Batter too dry.
- Under-manipulation (mixing).
- Pan too small.
- Oven temperature too low.
- Cake not baked through.
- Oven door opened during baking.
- Too much rising agent.
- Too much liquid.
- Batter left too long before baking.

**Cake rises and sinks in oven.**
- Too much liquid.
- Too much rising agent.
- Oven opened too soon or too often.

**Small brown speckles on surface of cake or biscuits.**
- Granulated sugar used instead of superfine sugar.

**Cake texture heavy.**
- Butter, sugar, and eggs not beaten together long enough.
- Flour stirred in too vigorously.
- Too much flour added to creamed mixture.
- Oven temperature too low.

**Coarse, grainy texture.**
- Too much rising agent.
- Insufficient creaming.
- Too much fat.

**Dry and crumbly texture.**
- Baked too long at low temperature.
- Too much rising agent.

**Tunnels and large holes.**
- Ingredients overmixed.
- Oven temperature too high.

**A dense and heavy cake texture.**
- Not enough air whisked into egg and sugar mixture.
- Flour not folded in gently enough.
- Oven temperature too low.

**Sunken fruit mixture.**
- Fruits wet or damp.
- Mixture too soft to support weight of fruit.

**Cracked top crust.**
- Mixture too stiff.
- Initial oven temperature too high.

**Overly browned crust.**
- Too much sugar.
- Oven temperature too high.

**Bitter or soapy aftertaste.**
- Too much baking powder/ baking soda.

## MUFFINS

**Muffins unevenly shaped.**
- Batter uneven in pans.
- Batter too runny.
- Batter not mixed enough.

**Muffins peak too high in center.**
- Overmixed batter.
- Too much flour.
- Too much baking powder.

**Muffins fell flat when taken out of oven.**
- Too little baking powder.
- Too much fat or sugar.
- Batter too thin.
- Pans too small.

**Muffins with tunnels.**
- Mixed for too long.
- Used an electric mixer.
- Too much baking powder.
- Oven temperature too high.

## PASTRIES

### Rolled-out pastries

**Pastry shrinks away from sides of the tart pan during baking.**
- Pastry stretched while being rolled out.
- Pastry not rested before and after being rolled.

**Pastry hard and tough.**
- Pastry overmixed in bowl or kneaded too much.
- Too much liquid added to rubbed-in flour and butter mixture.
- Too much flour used for dusting work counter when rolling out pastry.

### Choux pastry

**Pastry collapsed when removed from oven.**
- Pastry not baked for long enough.
- Hole not pierced through base of cooked pastry. Trapped steam caused pastry to go soft again.
- Oven temperature too high.

## COOKIES

**Cookies lose shape during baking.**
- Too much liquid.
- Dough not cool before baking.

**Too soft.**
- Not stored airtight.
- More than one type of cookie stored in container.

## BREADS

**Heavy bread.**
- Dough too stiff or soft.
- Insufficient proving time.
- Underbaked.

**Coarse texture.**
- Under-kneading.
- Excessive proving time.
- Dough too soft.
- Oven temperature too low.

**Small volume.**
- Too much sugar or fat.
- Insufficient proving time.
- Flour with poor gluten content.

**Uneven shape.**
- Bad shaping.
- Pan too small for amount of dough.
- Insufficient/excessive proving time.
- Pans too close together in oven.

**Cracked crust.**
- Dough too stiff.
- Insufficient proving time.
- Oven too hot.

## CORRECTING CAKE FLAWS
Use some of the following ideas:

### Petit Fours
Cut cake into 1¼-inch squares and sandwich together with apricot jelly. Pour over glacé icing and decorate.

### Tray bakes
Cut into squares, dip in frosting and roll in dry unsweetened coconut, chocolate vermicelli, or chopped nuts.

### Trifle
Use any offcuts for trifle. Fresh crumbs can also be used for trifle or any steamed puddings.

### Gâteau
Cut cake horizontally into three or four layers. Pour sherry, port, or brandy over and layer with custard, whipped cream, or any other fillings of choice. Decorate the cake with cream, chocolate, and any fruit of choice.

### Ring cake
When a cake has sunk in the center, cut the centre out and make a ring cake. Fill the ring with fresh fruit, and frost and decorate the cake.

# GLOSSARY

**ALMOND PASTE** A mixture of two-thirds sugar and one-third ground almonds combined with syrup or enough eggs to make a paste.

**BAKING BLIND** Baking a pie shell without a filling. The pastry is pricked all over with a fork, covered with waxed paper, and topped with dry beans (to retain the shape of the pastry during baking). It is baked for 5–10 minutes and then the beans and paper are removed.

**BAKING POWDER** A mixture containing baking soda, starch, and acids, used to make cakes and some light dough rise. The acids react with the baking soda when liquid is added, releasing the carbon dioxide that aerates the mixture.

**BAKING SODA** Sodium bicarbonate, an alkali that reacts with acids (such as buttermilk, yogurt, or cream of tartar) and releases carbon dioxide, which aerates the mixture.

**BEAT** To incorporate air into an ingredient or mixture by agitating it vigorously with a spoon, fork, whisk, or electric mixer.

**BLANCH** To immerse food briefly in boiling water to soften it (for example, vegetables), skin it (such as nuts), get rid of excess salt, or kill enzymes before freezing.

**BLEND** To fold or mix two or more ingredients together with a spoon, fork, whisk, or electric mixer.

**BOUQUET GARNI** Small bunch of herbs (often consisting of thyme, marjoram, parsley, and a bay leaf) tied together with string or placed in a small cheesecloth bag. Used to flavor soups and stews.

**BRAN** The outer layer or husk of the cereal grain; a major source of fiber.

**CARAMELIZE** To heat sugar or syrup slowly until brown in color (forms caramel).

**CONSISTENCY** The texture of a mixture, for example firm, dropping, or soft.

**CREAM OF TARTAR** Leavening acid with a rapid action to produce carbon dioxide. Used as the acid ingredient in some baking powders. It is added to candy and frosting mixtures for a creamier consistency, and to egg whites (such as meringue) before whisking to improve stability and volume and for a whiter color.

**CRÊPE** A thin, light pancake.

**CRYSTALLIZATION** When sugar that has been dissolved in a liquid forms crystals.

**CURDLE** To cause fresh milk, a sauce, or other liquid to separate into solids and liquids by overheating or by adding acid (such as lemon juice or vinegar), or to cause creamed butter and sugar to separate by adding the eggs too rapidly.

**DROPPING CONSISTENCY** The required texture of a cake or pudding mixture just before cooking. Test for it by taking a spoonful of the mixture and holding the spoon on its side above the bowl.

**DUMPLINGS** Small balls of dough, stuffing, or vegetable mixture, which are steamed or poached. They are used in puddings and to garnish soups and stews.

**DUST** To sprinkle flour on a work counter or inside a pan to prevent dough from sticking. Also to sprinkle lightly with flour, cornstarch, confectioner's sugar, and so on.

**ÉCLAIR** A long, hollow, finger-shaped puff made from choux pastry, filled with cream and topped with melted chocolate.

**EGG WASH** To brush on a mixture of fresh egg and water to put a shine on the crusts of breads and rolls.

**EXTRACT** Used for flavoring puddings and confectionery, made from natural or synthetic ingredients, or blends of both.

**FOLD IN** Combining a whisked or creamed mixture with other ingredients by cutting and folding so that it retains its lightness. A large metal spoon is used.

**FROSTING** The sweet coating on a cake or other baked item.

**FRY** To cook in fat or oil, either deep or shallow.

**GÂTEAU** A rich, decorated cake, often layered, which may include liqueur, cream, nuts, and fruit.

**GELATIN** Animal-derived gelling agent sold in powdered form or as leaf gelatine.

**GLAZE** To brush on a liquid to improve appearance and, sometimes, flavor. Ingredients for glazes include beaten egg, egg white, milk, syrup, and melted jelly.

**GLUTEN** The insoluble wheat protein left after hydration. This elastic substance assists in trapping carbon dioxide in bread dough. The strength of a flour's gluten determines its use. Bread dough requires a high gluten flour, while a cake mixture requires a low gluten, softer flour.

**GREASE** To apply a thin coating of fat or oil inside a cake, bread, or pie pan to prevent sticking.

**INCORPORATE** Mixing ingredients together in a recipe.

**KNEAD** To work ingredients into a mass of bread dough by mixing, usually by hand.

**MARZIPAN** A confection, made from almond paste, sugar, and egg whites, used for modeling fruits, figures, and so on.

**MERINGUE** Usually made by whisking egg whites with sugar. It is used for a topping or making shells and cookies.

**MIXING** Blending ingredients into a mass.

**MIXING TIME** This has a direct effect on leavening. Yeast, baking powder, and baking soda cannot do their jobs if the mixing time is incorrect. If dough or batter is overmixed and gets too hot, carbon dioxide will escape before the mixture is baked. Undermixing may cause uneven disbursement and dense grain, holes, and lack of volume.

**MOLASSES** A by-product of cane or beet sugar refinement.

**PASTRY BAG** A bag fitted with a tip which is used to pipe whipped cream, meringue, frosting, buttercreams or other pastes into neat, decorative shapes.

**PETIT FOURS** Tiny sponge cakes that have been frosted and decorated.

**PROVE** To let bread dough rise after shaping.

**PUNCH DOWN** The process of deflating a dough that has risen to ensure an even texture.

**PURÉE** Any fruit or vegetable rubbed through a sieve or worked in a blender or food processor until smooth.

**REDUCE** To thicken a sauce or other liquid by boiling rapidly in an open saucepan.

**RIND** The outer layer of citrus fruits that is finely grated to use as flavoring.

**RUB IN** Incorporating fat into flour when a short texture is required. Used for pastry, cakes, scones, and cookies. Rub with the fingertips to give a crumbly texture.

**SAUTÉ** Lightly fry in a small amount of oil or butter until golden.

**SIFT** To shake dry ingredients through a sifter to remove lumps, to aerate and to mix.

**SIMMER** To cook in liquid that is just below boiling point.

**SOUFFLÉ** A puffed up dish, made light by adding stiffly whisked egg white to a sauce or pureé (can be baked or steamed).

**VOL-AU-VENT** A light, flaky case of puff pastry with a lid, filled with a sweet or savoury mixture.

# INDEX

Page numbers in *italics* refer to photographs.

**Baking**
equipment 9
mistakes 124-125
rules 8-9
trays and pans 9
sizes 9
**Bars, slices, and sweet treats, recipes**
apricot bars, chewy 28, *29*
banana-oat squares 120, *121*
brandy snap rolls 28
brownies, decadent 24, *25*
butterhorns 22
caramel apple pieces, sticky 26, *27*
cherry balls 28, *29*
cherry dream bars 22, *23*
chocolate-coconut slices 28, *29*
chocolate-nut squares 22
coconut ice slices 120, *121*
coconut jelly squares 122, *123*
cupcakes, vanilla 118
fairy cakes (var.) 118
éclairs, granadilla 26, *27*
ginger squares 24, *25*
granola bars 24, *25*
koeksisters 29
peanut and raisin squares 118
truffles 26, *27*
**Bread, roll, and bun recipes**
basil and bell pepper cornbread 50, *51*
caramel-pecan buns 52, *53*
cheese bread, Italian-style 48, *49*
ciabatta rolls 57, *57*
fruit bread, spicy 54, *55*
granary bread, seeded 48, *49*
honey oat bread 52, *53*
hot cross buns 110, *111*
mealie bread 56, *57*
pita breads 50, *51*

pot bread 52, *53*
roosterkoek (var.) 52, *53*
rolls, soft 54
plaited bread (var.) 54, *55*
scallion and garlic rolls 50, *51*
spinach and cheese plait *47*, 48
stollen 113, *113*
tomato and onion cottage bread 56, *57*
yogurt bread 56, *57*
**Breads**
baking 46
kneading and proving 46
mixing 46
punching down and second rising 46
storing 46
types of 46
buttercream frosting 110

**Cakes**
storing 30
testing guidelines 30
**Cakes, large and loaves, recipes**
apple loaf 45, *45*
apricot-almond cake 42, *43*
banana loaf 32, *33*
basic sponge for novelty cakes 118, *119*
Battenburg cake 112, *113*
beet and carrot cake 38, *39*
butter cake 40, *41*
chocolate cake (var.) 40
nut cake (var.) 40
orange cake (var.) 40
passion fruit cake (var.) 40
spice cake (var.) 40
buttermilk cake 36
buttermilk chocolate cake, moist 44, *45*
carrot cake 40, *41*

cheesecake, ultimate 42, *43*
chocolate (var.) 42, *43*
chocolate cake, moist dark 41
coconut loaf, Madeira 32, *33*
fruitcake, dark 106, *109*
honey cake 38
jelly roll, apricot 34
chocolate (var.) 34
lemon loaf 38, *39*
meringue cake *31*, 44
orange and zucchini loaf 34, *35*
peanut butter loaf 40, *41*
pineapple cake 32, *33*
pineapple fruitcake 112
poppy seed delight 36, *37*
prune cake 36, *37*
Sachertorte 114, *115*
sherry and orange cake 106
sour cream cinnamon cake 34, *35*
spiral cake *107*, 110
sponge cake, hot milk 118
chocolate (var.) 118
sweet potato loaf 37, *37*
tiramisu gâteau *111*, 114
conversion tables 8, 9
**Cookie recipes**
almond cookies, rich 14, *15*
butterscotch cookies 14, *15*
cheesy barbecue cookies 18, *19*
cherry-pistachio biscotti 108, *109*
chocolate cookies, fruity 120, *121*
chocolate chip cookies, rich 18, *19*
chocolate chunk cookies 10, *11*
Christmas almond cookies 114, *115*

Christmas shape cookies 115, *115*
cottage delights 12, *13*
crunchies 14
gingerbread men 122
ginger cookies 15, *15*
gumdrop cookies 123, *123*
jelly and coconut cookies 12, *13*
melting moments 14
oat and raisin cookies, spicy 16
peanut butter cookies 116
rocky road cookies 116, *117*
shortbread 62
millionaire's 18, *19*
traditional 16, *17*
twirls 12, *13*
chocolate (var.) 12
spicy cookies 18, *19*
surprise bites 16, *17*
herb biscuits (var.) 16
**Cookies**
baking 10
storing 10
types of
dropped 10
refrigerator 10
rolled 10
shaped 10
crêpes 92, 102, 126
crumpets 116
custard, orange liqueur 108

**Dessert recipes**
apple and carrot pudding 105, *105*
apple crumble, spicy 96
apricot steamed pudding 98, *99*
buttermilk pudding 100
chocolate fudge pudding 100, *101*
crêpes, creamy banana, with

caramel *97*, 102
date pudding, sticky 100, *101*
dumplings, golden 96
fritters, pumpkin, with
	caramel sauce 102, *103*
fruity pudding 96
ginger pudding 98, *99*
individual brandy puddings
	104
lemon-semolina pudding
	100, *101*
malva pudding 102, *103*
pear and ginger roly-poly
	104, *105*
pineapple and coconut
	pudding 98, *99*
plum pudding 108, *109*

Frosting
basic 30, 118
butter 40, *41*
caramel 37
chocolate 44, 118
cream cheese 36, 40
glacé icing 115
lemon 36
royal icing 106

glaze, sugar 54

Ingredients 4-7
baking powder 7, 125
baking soda 7, 125
butter 6
	baking 6
	storing 6
	substituting 6
eggs 7
	baking 7
	storing 7
	substituting 7
flour 4-5
	all-purpose 4, *5*
	bread flour 5, *5*
	digestive bran 5, *5*
	granary flour 5, *5*
	non-wheat flours 5-6
	wheat bran 5, *5*
	wheat germ flour 5, *5*

self-rising flour 5, *5*
semolina 5, *5*
spelt flour 5
storing 4
substituting 6
sugar 6
	confectioner's sugar 6
	granulated sugar 6
	muscovado sugar 7
	raw brown sugar 7
	soft brown sugar 6
	superfine sugar 6
yeast 7

marzipan 106, 126
meringue 44, 126
mince pies 112, *113*
Muffin recipes
	apricot, orange, and
		buttermilk 72, *73*
	bacon-cheddar 72, *73*
	banana-cinnamon 70
	blueberry, best-ever 72, *73*
	bran, healthy 76, *77*
	cappuccino 76
		double chocolate (var.) 76
	carrot, spicy 74, *75*
	cheese, bell pepper, and
		mushroom 70, *71*
		ham and tomato (var.) 70
	citrus 74, *75*
	honey-granola 74, *75*
	mandarin 76, *77*
Muffins
	cooling 70
	freezing 70
	mixing 70

Ovens 9
	temperatures 9

pancakes, basic 102
Pastry
	baking blind 58, 125
	glazing 58
	mixing 58
	rolling out 58
	shaping 58
	types of

cheese 94
choux 8
cream cheese 8, 92
flaky 7
puff 7, 80
pie dough 7, 95
rich pie dough 7, 66, 68, 69
soda-water 8, 112
sweet pie dough 7
Pie shells
	almond 64
	coconut 64
	potato 88
	sweet potato 92
Pies and main course bakes
	recipes
	asparagus pie, crustless
		84, *85*
	bacon plait, creamy 80, *81*
	bobotie pie 92, *93*
	cheese and chile puffs 86, *87*
	cheese and herb puffs
		122, *123*
	chicken and pasta pie 84, *85*
	chicken strips, crumbed
		86, *87*
	chicken wraps, tandoori
		88, *89*
	chive-onion twists 80
	crêpes, ratatouille 92, *93*
	fish pie 88, *89*
	fritters
		bacon 84, *85*
		camembert 87, *87*
		zucchini 90, *91*
	ground beef pie with cobbler
		topping 90, *91*
	ground beef vetkoekies
		90, *91*
	leek pies 92, *93*
	onion rings in batter
		88, *89*
	pizza, ground beef 94, *95*
	pork pie, fruity 82, *83*
	potato bake 86
	quiche, vegetable 94, *95*
	spinach pie 95, *95*
	venison and bacon pie
		82, *83*

play dough 120

Rusk recipes
	bran, light 20, *21*
	buttermilk 20
	buttermilk-coconut 20
	butternut 21, *21*
	granola 20, *21*

Sauces
	caramel 102
	cinnamon brandy 108
Scone recipes
	buttermilk 79
		cheese (var.) 79
		date or nut (var.) 79
		herb (var.) 79
	cheddar-dill 78, *79*
	fruit 78, *79*
	orange-pumpkin 78, *79*
Sweet tarts and pies,
	recipes
	almond-pear pie *59*, 60
	apple custard pie 62, *63*
	apple tart 60, *61*
	banana-caramel tartlets,
		creamy 66, *67*
	caramel-peppermint tart
		64, *65*
	coconut milk tart, crustless
		60, *61*
	coconut tart, Greek 58
	fig tart, green 62, *63*
	frangipane tart 69, *69*
	ginger and cherry sponge pie
		68, *69*
	lemon tart, creamy 68. *69*
		lemon meringue (var.) 68
	mango and passion fruit
		pie 64, *65*
	milk tart, quick 64, *65*
	pineapple pie 66, *67*